PRAISE FOR *GIVING VOICES TO VALUES IN THE BOARDROOM*

Professor Clark's outstanding and much-needed book, *Giving Voices to Values in the Boardroom*, starts from the premise that voicing one's values matters to board decision-making, and values drive behavior. To change behaviors, director voices are needed.

Speaking up can be very challenging – and even costly – for directors.

Beginning with the central challenge in corporate governance – director independence – Dr. Clark critiques real boardroom situations that both strengthen and undermine director independence, competencies and dynamics. Then, Dr. Clark proceeds to tackle the central role of a board: CEO succession and compensation, and linking both of these to strategic execution. Dr. Clark concludes with the risks and opportunities of digitization, which has the power not only to disrupt business models but make companies obsolete. Again, voices matter. A good board is never in denial.

Based on weaving research with real board situations and interviews, Professor Clark's book is a welcome and fresh perspective on the way boards actually impact performance (or not). This book makes a significant contribution to the field and should be a must-have for any director who wants to make a difference on the board on which they are a member. I highly recommend it!

—**Richard Leblanc**, FCMC, BSc, MBA, LLB, JD, LLM, PhD
Professor of Governance, Law & Ethics, York University, and Independent Advisor to Boards

GIVING VOICE TO VALUES IN THE BOARDROOM

This book takes the central issues facing board members today and applies the giving voice to values framework while also providing insights from practicing board members who have faced these issues. It covers such topics as strategic planning and monitoring, director independence, privacy and cyber risk, executive compensation and CEO succession planning. With this book, readers will also grapple with the conflicts of interest that might arise in the director selection process, role of the nominating committee and the compensation committee in order to cultivate more optimal board dynamics.

The principles of giving voice to values start by asking a deceptively simple question: '*What if you were going to act on your values—what would you say and do?*' The book then provides an overview of the current landscape of corporate governance along with the major rules and director duties applicable to the board of directors. The book's latter chapters contain a series of five scenarios common to the board of directors that are presented as a set of "Board Challenges" involving the tensions often found in board work.

In *Giving Voice to Values in the Boardroom*, the author, Cynthia E. Clark, provides practical strategies for board members and other constituents of corporate governance to deal with these challenges. These cases are designed to help users of the book implement prescripting and action planning. Each case will also have discussion questions about the stakes and stakeholders, common reasons and rationalizations and examples of how firms and governance professionals have handled similar board challenges.

Cynthia E. Clark, Ph.D is a corporate governance and business ethics expert focusing on shareholder activism, ESG issues, proxy disclosures and data privacy. She has also conducted training sessions on ethical decision-making and optimal nominating and governance procedures to numerous senior management teams and boards of directors. She is widely cited in the media on governance issues, including recently in *The Wall Street Journal*, *The Boston Globe*, CNN, Reuters and multiple appearances on Bloomberg Radio. She is an active member and speaker with the National Association of Corporate Directors, 2020 Women on Boards and the Society for Governance Professionals. She is the author of *Business & Society: Ethical, Legal and Digital Environments*. Cynthia is also a Professor of Management at Bentley University and Director of the Geneen Institute for Corporate Governance.

Giving Voice to Values

Series Editor: Mary C. Gentile

The *Giving Voice to Values* series is a collection of books on Business Ethics and Corporate Social Responsibility that brings a practical, solutions-oriented, skill-building approach to the salient questions of values-driven leadership.

Giving Voice to Values (GVV: www.GivingVoiceToValues.org) – the curriculum, the pedagogy and the research upon which it is based – was designed to transform the foundational assumptions upon which the teaching of business ethics is based, and importantly, to equip future business leaders to know not only what is right – but how to make it happen.

Giving Voice to Values as a Professional Physician
Ira Bedzow

Authentic Excellence
R. Kelly Crace and Robert L. Crace

Ethics, CSR and Sustainability (ECSRS) Education in the Middle East and North Africa (MENA) Region
Edited by Noha El-Bassiouny, Dina El-Bassiouny, Ehab K. A. Mohamed, and Mohamed A. K. Basuony

Engaging the Heart in Business
Alice Alessandri and Alberto Aleo

Shaping the Future of Work: A Handbook for Building a New Social Contract
Thomas A. Kochan and Lee Dyer

Professionalism and Values in Law Practice
Robert Feldman

Giving Voice to Values in the Boardroom
Cynthia E. Clark

GIVING VOICE TO VALUES IN THE BOARDROOM

Cynthia E. Clark

LONDON AND NEW YORK

First published 2021
by Routledge
2 Park Square, Milton Park, Abingdon, Oxon OX14 4RN

and by Routledge
52 Vanderbilt Avenue, New York, NY 10017

Routledge is an imprint of the Taylor & Francis Group, an informa business

British Library Cataloguing-in-Publication Data
A catalogue record for this book is available from the British Library

Library of Congress Cataloging-in-Publication Data
Names: Clark, Cynthia E., author.
Title: Giving voice to values in the boardroom / Cynthia E. Clark.
Description: First Edition. | New York : Routledge, 2021. | Series: Giving voice to values | Includes bibliographical references and index. | Identifiers: LCCN 2020036052 (print) | LCCN 2020036053 (ebook) | ISBN 9780367179373 (hardback) | ISBN 9780367179397 (paperback) | ISBN 9780367179397 (ebook)
Subjects: LCSH: Corporate governance. | Social responsibility of business. | Directors of corporations. | Business ethics.
Classification: LCC HD2741 .C455 2021 (print) | LCC HD2741 (ebook) | DDC 658.4/22–dc23
LC record available at https://lccn.loc.gov/2020036052
LC ebook record available at https://lccn.loc.gov/2020036053

ISBN: 978-0-367-17937-3 (hbk)
ISBN: 978-0-367-17939-7 (pbk)
ISBN: 978-0-429-05854-7 (ebk)

Typeset in Joanna
by KnowledgeWorks Global Ltd.

DEDICATION

To Roberta P. Clark, the lead director of our family who always voices her values

CONTENTS

ACKNOWLEDGMENTS

I am greatly indebted to Mary Gentile, whose book *Giving Voice to Values* not only inspired me to deepen the discussion of values in corporate governance but who also provided terrific insight, direction and enthusiasm for the idea. My senior editor Rebecca Marsh also provided invaluable guidance. I am grateful to Bentley University which gave me the time and support necessary for the completion of this book.

I am especially grateful to a number of board directors who agreed to be interviewed for this book providing a richness to each of the board challenges. Each one continues to strive to work toward exemplifying the very principles mentioned in this book. My colleagues at the Society for Governance Professionals, the National Association of Corporate Directors and the International Corporate Governance Network have also provided valuable input and networking opportunities.

Importantly, I would like to thank my son Brendan for his unwavering interest and support in what I do.

ABBREVIATIONS

AI	Artificial intelligence
COVID-19	Coronavirus disease 2019
CCPA	California Consumer Privacy Act
CD&A	Compensation Discussion and Analysis
CII	Council of Institutional Investors
ESG	Environmental, social and governance
FTC	U.S. Federal Trade Commission
GDPR	General Data Protection Regulation
GVV	Giving Voice to Values
LTIs	Long-term incentives
NACD	National Association of Corporate Directors
ICGN	International Corporate Governance Network
ISG	Investor Stewardship Group
ISS	Institutional Shareholder Services
NC	Nominating committee
NYSE	New York Stock Exchange
OECD	Organization for Economic Cooperation and Development
PI	Personal information
SEC	U.S. Securities & Exchange Commission

STIs Short-term incentives
TDC Total direct compensation
TSR Total shareholder return
RDA Relative degree of alignment
WEF World Economic Forum

GIVING VOICE TO VALUES IN THE BOARDROOM

By Cynthia E. Clark PhD

Introduction

The corporate governance of firms and the role of the board of directors are at a crossroads. On the one hand, they have never been more vital to the workings of a business. On the other, they have never been more challenging. As boards grapple with new regulations about transparency and accountability, ongoing sustainability concerns, executive pay and performance challenges, the rights of shareholders and other stakeholders, and the aftermath of COVID-19, just to name a few, it's easy to see that board work is inherently value-driven. Simply put, boards must both focus on the moral element as well as the legal aspects of their role.

Giving voice to values (GVV) is an established framework for just this type of value-centered context and therefore it is an ideal lens easily and effectively applied to the everyday concerns of individual board members and to the board as a whole. GVV is about implementation – or the action one takes – where a person knows what his or her values are.

Specifically, our emphasis will be on preparing what we will say, our script, and the best approach to implement it rather than debating what is or is not ethical. Therefore, the focus in this book is on developing the necessary skills (e.g., problem-solving and reframing, data gathering, relationship building, sequencing conversations and actions) for what you could say and do and how you can make those efforts most effective.

This book takes the central issues facing board members today and applies the GVV framework to them while also providing insights from practicing board members who have faced these issues. We'll cover topics such as strategic planning and monitoring, fiduciary duties, privacy and data usage, executive compensation and succession planning. We'll also grapple with the conflicts of interest that might arise in the *director selection process*, role of the *nominating committee* and the *compensation committee* as well as the cultivation of more optimal board dynamics.[1]

The best way to use this book is to share it with your board and work through the challenges presented. Another option would be to work on these during a working dinner with an outside expert. All directors should read Parts 1 and 2 in their entirety as they lay the groundwork. Part 1 explains the GVV framework and Part 2 provides an overview of the landscape of corporate governance along with the major rules and director duties applicable to the board of directors. Part 3 contains a set of five scenarios common to the board of directors that are presented as a set of "Board Challenges" involving the tensions inherent in fulfilling board work. These scenarios focus on board independence, the nominating committee and director selection, CEO succession and compensation and data privacy:

1. *Board Challenge #1*: Independence and the Gray Director
2. *Board Challenge #2*: What is our Director Selection Process?
3. *Board Challenge #3*: CEO Succession and Planning for the Future
4. *Board Challenge #4*: CEO Compensation and the Rising Star
5. *Board Challenge #5*: Cybersecurity or Digital Innovation?

Each scenario weaves together real events, albeit disguised, board of director interviews, press coverage of specific board interactions, decisions or behaviors as well as current research in corporate governance. Each board challenge is designed to be used by your board as an iterative learning exercise.

The overall goal in presenting these scenarios is to prescript and prepare an action plan for a value-driven position through the eyes of a protagonist. After articulating the position and anticipating the "push back", the protagonist is likely to encounter, the GVV materials identify the most common categories of these objections and suggest tactics for crafting responses to them. The intention in reading these scenarios, preparing scripts, and discussing strategies with peers, is that you will be better equipped to address ethical situations when they arise in the course of your work as a board director.

Keep in mind, these scenarios are designed to be "post-decision-making", meaning each director profiled in them has already identified what he or she believes is the right course of action. For example, a director knows he or she must address the increasing lack of independence on their board. Given this, GVV focuses on how to get that accomplished and, in fact, there are typically more ways than one to navigate the challenge. In general, the question we routinely asked is: "*How does the director act on what s/he believes is right – effectively*"?

My goal is to help individual directors and boards figure out the optimal board of director behaviors, tasks and roles while learning how to cultivate them and improve board dynamics. The answers lie in using the GVV framework alongside my 20+ years of working with boards and conducting research in the corporate governance arena. Insights from my consulting work inform the board challenges presented and the set of leading practices in handling them.

Note

1. Definitions are provided for words in italics throughout this book.

PART 1

THE GIVING VOICE TO VALUES (GVV) FRAMEWORK

1

THE GVV FRAMEWORK

What are values?

The central premise behind giving voice to values (GVV) is that individuals can increase the likelihood of acting on their values – and the efficacy when they do so – by learning a predetermined framework and then practicing how to use that framework when values conflicts arise.[1] It can be summed up as building a *moral muscle memory* so that when issues inevitably arise, they are better prepared.

All board members face ethical dilemmas. These ethical dilemmas are most often about conflicts with moral values. By values, we don't mean qualities like "creativity" or "innovation" – which are important no doubt – but rather moral values that are widely shared across time and culture. In fact, the GVV framework makes an important distinction between ethics and values. Ethics are ruled-based and externally imposed. Values are personal and deeply held beliefs about good and bad behavior, desirable and undesirable actions, right versus wrong.[2]

By focusing on values, the GVV framework allows individuals to speak from a self-motivated, aspirational position rather than an obligatory stance imposed from the outside. Board members are uniquely poised to speak from such a position as they are endowed with the highest authority in firm decision-making.[3]

A great deal of academic research argues that senior executives see their decision situations through personalized lenses formed by their experiences, personalities and values.[4] These different value systems not only give rise to conflicts between board members but also lead to different company and board practices.

You may be thinking there must be a very wide range of values making it difficult to voice your values in the boardroom. However, research across cultures and different time periods shows there are five widely shared values: honesty, respect, responsibility, fairness and compassion.[5]

These values often conflict with some other compelling option (e.g., profit, market share, promotion) or a fear, such as being fired, marginalized or otherwise retaliated against. We all face these types of situations where we are tempted by these other attractive options. Still, we can understand and even normalize temptations in the business world without accepting them as being appropriate.

In fact, conflicting values are *not* choices between having values and not having values. Instead, tensions arise typically in two settings:

1. They sometimes arise because there is a conflict between two important values: maybe telling the truth or being fair to your fellow directors. In this situation, because two important values are involved or both choices can be expressed as a value, we tend to think both choices are equally good. But that is rarely the case.
2. There can also be a conflict between a moral value and a temptation that many of your fellow board members advocate for. This latter type is usually framed as a choice between what is right and what is essentially a well-crafted rationalization of a wrong. We will discuss rationalizations in the next section.

As personal and organizational values come into focus in our daily life, according to the GVV approach, it is useful to become somewhat familiar, even comfortable, with the idea that recognizing and communicating them is a normal part of business – in fact many experts believe it is a must.[6] However, any business decision comes with a risk that it will not turn out like we hoped it would. So, unfortunately, our choices come with no guarantees.[7] Yet there are times when a clear wrong is in full view and the GVV framework focuses on how to address it, especially when we feel unable to act, but are nevertheless interested in trying to figure out how to enact effectively.

These are the types of conversations about values – and acting on them – we address in this book. Before doing that, however, we need to look into the GVV process and become aware of the roadblocks. Still, it's important to keep in mind recognizing our differences does not preclude boards from developing or even pursuing shared goals which can act as a preliminary position for thinking more about how to voice and act on those values down the road.[8]

Tale of two stories

Before we move on, let's take a closer look at the power of choice – or what GVV calls the *tale of two stories*. This is a brief exercise to help us clarify who we are, who we've been, and who we can be.[9] The exercise is simple because it relies on our past experiences at work.

Each board director should answer both these stories on his or her own.

Story 1, speaking up

Recall a time at work when your values conflicted with what you were expected to do regarding a nontrivial board decision and you spoke up and acted to resolve the conflict in a way that was consistent with your values.

- Describe the situation.
- What did you do and what was the impact?
- What motivated you to speak up and act?
- What made it easier for you to speak up – things in your control or in others' control?

Story 2, not speaking up

Recall a time at work when your values conflicted with what you were expected to do regarding a nontrivial board decision and you did *not* speak up to resolve the conflict in a way that was consistent with your values.

- Describe the situation.
- Why didn't you speak up or act?

- What would have motivated you to speak up and act?
- What would have made it easier to speak up – things in your control or in others' control?

By juxtaposing these two stories, we are better able to define our motivations and inhibitors but also those of the companies on whose board we serve. In effect, we can create a list of both *enablers* and *disablers* that affect our ability to voice our values. Bringing these types of work memories to the front of your mind and revisiting the tale of two stories is a skill and confidence builder. Building moral muscle memory involves this type of reflection so that when a similar business context or personal situation comes up, we can more easily recognize it and deal with it effectively.

Rationalizations

Sometimes it's difficult to talk about our values and immediately change the behaviors of ourselves or others because, typically, our inner thoughts and emotions (i.e., cognition and affect) present us with a rather sophisticated set of rationalizations for either acting or not.

Drawing on the actual experience of business practitioners as well as social science and management research, author Mary Gentile developed the GVV framework to help managers combat rationalizations so they may voice their values. According to Gentile, a manager must ask, "What if I were going to act on my values – what would I say and do?"[10] GVV provides a framework for answering this question so a manager can practice, script and then act on his or her values in the workplace.

There are a number of common rationalizations in business contexts and in this book I apply them to the board of directors. For example, we might face the (1) standard practice/status quo, (2) materiality, (3) locus of responsibility and (4) locus of loyalty rationalizations. These are by no means a full set of rationalizations you might encounter in your company or board. But it's helpful to explain in detail these commonly experienced ones so when you do encounter these types of pushback, you are better prepared to work on your action plan.

The standard practice argument is best captured by the statement, "Everyone does it". This argument assumes that an action is acceptable simply because the majority of the people engage in it or because it is something that has been done for a long period of time. This rationalization is powerful and many of us use it to avoid taking responsibility. Such a rationalization might apply, for example, to a board's use of pay consultants to determine Chief Executive Officer (CEO) pay and subsequently ratchet it up.

Second, the rationalization of materiality refers to making the argument, to yourself or others, that an action is not material – that is, it doesn't matter, it is insubstantial, it does not hurt anyone or it does not make a difference in the long run. Framing the question in terms of materiality shifts the focus from the action to its consequences, and it also minimizes those consequences. Here, people tend to believe that if they can live with the consequences of an act, then it is acceptable. Consequences, however, tend to multiple and are often not known fully at the time. Using this rationalization, you might hear people saying, "*It's no big deal*" or "*It's not that important to the overall picture*". For example, such a rationalization might apply to hiring a new board member who is personally connected to the firm in some way.

A third customary rationalization involves one's locus of responsibility. Responsibility refers to our sense of who we think *should* act in a given situation or who is requiring us to act in a situation. We tell ourselves either "*It is not my problem*" or "*I'm just following orders*". This rationalization usually reduces your personal accountability because you think your actions result from some authority figure who has the control. Perhaps you've heard a board member say they are just following orders (of the committee, of the CEO, etc.). Sometimes we hear people claim they are not the appropriate person to handle the situation or do not possess the requisite authority to remedy the issue or are simply following directions. Sometimes we extend this rationalization to blaming the victim of harm for a variety of reasons – "*It's their own fault*".

Fourth, we justify actions that concern the locus of loyalty. Needless to say, our loyalties can conflict. We can, at the same time, want to be fair to one person but also not want to harm another. This rationalization assumes that loyalty to one group necessarily means disloyalty to another group. For example, a fellow director might ask you not to reveal his devotion to the CEO when making board decisions. He is loyal to the CEO but not loyal to the process of objective decision-making incumbent upon the board, another form of loyalty. Sometimes, people express this rationalization something like "*I don't want to harm [person x] but I know this isn't fair to [person y]*". It is important to note this rationalization is not the same as a director's duty of loyalty discussed at length in a later section.

Each of these rationalizations can be identified and worked through. In doing so, it doesn't mean we will become free of personal bias or ethical temptations. It does mean we will recognize them more quickly and begin to implement change. GVV is not just about the cognitive process of awareness and analysis of these rationalizations, but, even more, it is about the prescripting and rehearsal – the creation of a *moral muscle memory* – so that these responses are more natural, comfortable, even automatic. Much of current research suggests that we react to ethical conflicts emotionally, immediately, automatically, rather than initially thinking them through rationally.[11] So, we need to create an alternate automatic response based on our values through practice.

What is giving voice?

Voice is important for promoting effective team functioning, and a board is one of the most vital teams in a company. Voice can often ensure the board has up-to-date and relevant information, better preparation for strategic change and a more complete set of alternatives.[12]

Therefore, pushing back on these rationalizations and developing our automatic response involves considering how to effectively use your voice – ideally without being perceived as self-righteous. You might ask then, what do we mean by *voicing* your values? First, a few clarifications are as follows:

1. Voice is not only about speaking up.
2. Both voice and loyalty can coexist.
3. Voice and exit are not exclusive alternatives.

It would certainly be reasonable to assume that voicing our values is merely about speaking up – or whistleblowing – when we see conflicts of interest or dishonest behaviors in our firm. However, giving voice may also mean asking a well-constructed question, offering a new way of thinking about a situation, providing additional analyses or finding another way to accomplish a task that is more acceptable ethically. Voice also involves taking the needs, desires, and emotional investments of others into consideration – in effect about finding ways to talk about values successfully. By anticipating or listening to others' concerns, you will be better able to find a mutually acceptable way to address the situation. So, in fact, voice may be soft or loud and is by no means always an overt protest.[13] A useful way of thinking of voice is the discretionary communication of work-related ideas, suggestions, concerns or opinions.[14]

Second, we acknowledge the very real possibility that loyalty can be a form of action which coexists alongside using one's voice. In other words, a board member may voice her values *because* he or she is loyal to the firm rather than in spite of it. Often, however, voicing our values can be perceived as being *dis*loyal to our friends or our colleagues. Many people assume the greater the extent to which we identify with the organization, the greater the likelihood our perceptions are distorted in ways favorable to the firm – meaning we believe we must avoid the label "not committed to the firm". This assumption relies on a false dichotomy, as if unethical behavior and loyalty to the firm are one and the same. Loyalty does not mean doing anything our company wants us to do. Likewise, it differs from a board member's duty of loyalty (discussed in depth in p. 30 "Duties of the Board"), where a board member's personal interests must remain secondary to that of his or her board work.

However, part of learning to voice our values is to frame words like "loyalty" in different ways so that loyalty does not cloud our perception or replace thinking. In reframing this false "loyalty versus integrity" challenge, we acknowledge that being loyal to our friends and colleagues occurs when we stand up to them in voicing our honest values and beliefs. For example, we can define loyalty as being transparent with colleagues about our obligations and principles as board members. We can talk about loyalty as the type of loyalty to a different vision of our board or of our culture – one that is both successful and honest. We must also consider loyalty to other important relationships. Our selves? Our family? Which one do you feel the greatest loyalty to?

Third, the tendency to leave a firm – often termed "exit" – is sometimes chosen instead of voicing one's concerns. Often, exit and voice are positioned as exclusive alternatives – meaning you must do one or the other.[15] However, this form of exit is likely to have little effect on the organization. And even if you decide to exit, it can and often should be accompanied by voice. Thus, it is possible to use voice and exit simultaneously. Additionally, you can exit a task but not the board, a sort of soft exit if you will.

Some additional consideration should be given to the firm's organizational culture. Some companies are easier to speak up than others. Factors such as the levels of hierarchy, the communication systems and the leadership styles of top management can influence the workplace context. Although a more closed and rigid organizational structure does not excuse you from voicing your values, it does inform the strategy you might use to raise ethical discussions.

Finally, it is vital to recognize the common reasons and rationalizations, just introduced above, that people use in boardrooms for following a particular course of action or for choosing to remain silent.

Using prescripting

As discussed above, GVV is about data gathering, problem reframing, building relationships, finding allies, etc., and the use of prescripting is the culmination of the above thinking exercises of the GVV framework. At hso that you can respond to common reasons and rationalizations. Some responses are predictable; others may be anticipated only after considering a series of questions. Either way, by thinking through the responses you are likely to receive, you can construct counterarguments. It also helps avoid being caught off guard, which can result in unnecessary tension, emotional reactions or stereotypical accusations. Being prepared helps you to act calmly and rationally when responding to the barriers others try to place in your way.

But being prepared does not mean being perfect. Your approach and your script will never be perfect. There will be responses and reactions you did not anticipate. You have to be willing to make peace with imperfection, prepare for what you can and move forward rather than risk not acting because you are trying to shore up every possible argument. Prescripting is not meant to imply your audience will be more receptive to your arguments. You will likely face the same opposition; however, you will be speaking from a position of strength, confidence and clarity. And, ideally, you will be able to keep the conversation going, hopefully to a better resolution, rather than simply being shut down by the rationalizations you encounter initially. For this reason, we often use a decision tree to accommodate the need to redirect.

The questions you need to think about, in general, are the following as you craft an action plan and a script for the five board challenges presented later in the book. First, place yourself in the center of the situation and in the shoes of the protagonist: what should you say, to whom, when and how? Second, think about how others on the board may see the situation: is it different or similar? In order to answer these questions, consider the following:

- What are the main arguments you (or they) are trying to counter? That is, what are the *reasons and rationalizations* you (they) need to address?
- What's at *stake* for the key parties, including those who disagree with you? How can you find allies among those who may agree with you? Does anyone agree with you? (Inside the board? Outside the board?)
- What is your (his or her) most powerful and persuasive response to the reasons and rationalizations needing to be addressed? To whom should the argument be made? When and in what context?

Each board challenge gives you or your board the opportunity to prepare and critique a script for that challenge. And, these exercises provide a good use of time at a board meeting, working dinner or retreat to help strengthen the board's culture and decision-making.

Notes

1. Gentile, M. C. (2010). *Giving voice to values: How to speak your mind when you know what's right.* Ann Arbor, MI: McGraw-Hill Companies, Inc.
2. Zak, P. J. (2008). *Moral markets: The critical role of values in the economy.* Princeton, New Jersey: Princeton University Press.
3. See Forbes, D. P., & Milliken, F. J. (1999). Cognition and corporate governance: Understanding boards of directors as strategic decision-making groups. *Academy of Management Review, 24*(3), 489–505.
4. Hambrick, D. C., & Mason, P. A. (1984). Upper echelons: The organization as a reflection of its top managers. *Academy of Management Review, 9*(2), 193–206. See also Chin, M. K., Hambrick, D. C., & Treviño, L. K. (2013). Political ideologies of CEOs: The influence of executives' values

on corporate social responsibility. *Administrative Science Quarterly, 58*(2), 197–232.

5. Kidder, R. (2005). *Moral courage: Taking action when your values are put to the test.* New York, NY: William Morrow.
6. For example, leadership experts Brene Brown and Simon Sinek believe it is a must. See https://storiesincorporated.com/when-human-values-and-organizational-values-overlap/
7. Gentile, M. C. (2010). *Giving voice to values: How to speak your mind when you know what's right.* Ann Arbor, MI: McGraw-Hill Companies, Inc., chp. 4.
8. Gentile, M. C. (2010). *Giving voice to values: How to speak your mind when you know what's right.* Ann Arbor, MI: McGraw-Hill Companies, Inc., chp. 2.
9. This section and exercise are based on Gentile, M.C. (2010). Giving voice to values: How to speak your mind when you know what's right. Ann Arbor, MI: McGraw-Hill Companies, Inc., chp. 3.
10. Gentile, M. C. (2010). Giving voice to values: How to speak your mind when you know what's right. Ann Arbor, MI: McGraw-Hill Companies, Inc., p. xxxv.
11. Haidt, J. (2001). The emotional dog and its rational tail: A social intuitionist approach to moral judgment. *Psychological Review, 108*(4), 814.
12. Edmondson, A. C. (2003). Speaking up in the operating room: How team leaders promote learning in interdisciplinary action teams. *Journal of Management Studies,* 40(6): 1419–1452. Edmondson, A. C. (2012). Teamwork on the fly. *Harvard Business Review,* 90(4), 72–80.
13. In contrast to Hirschman, A. O. (1972). *Exit, voice, and loyalty: Responses to decline in firms, organizations and states.* Cambridge: Harvard University Press; and Kolarska, L., & Aldrich, H. (1980). Exit, voice, and silence: Consumers' and managers' responses to organizational decline. *Organization Studies, 1*(1), 41–58.
14. Morrison, E. W. (2011). Employee voice behavior: Integration and directions for future research. *Academy of Management Annals, 5,* 373–412.
15. See Hirschman (1972).

PART 2

CORPORATE GOVERNANCE

A pursuit and a profession

2

CORPORATE GOVERNANCE

What is corporate governance?

Interestingly, the term *corporate governance* tends to mean different things to different people having evolved somewhat over time. This evolution is a result of both regulation and various crises. Broadly speaking, corporate governance specifies the distribution of rights and responsibilities among various corporate participants including board members, executives, shareholders and other stakeholders; it spells out the rules and procedures for making decisions on corporate affairs.[1]

A great body of corporate governance literature is dedicated to the alignment of objectives between the board of directors and a firm's shareholders. This perspective – examining the monitoring role of boards of directors – focuses on the challenge related to the separation of ownership and control.[2] Under this perspective, the organization is faced with an agency problem in which the principal (i.e., shareholders of a company) delegates responsibility to the agent (i.e., company executives) and forgoes part of its control in the decision-making process (see Figure 2.1).

Effective monitoring and control of top management, therefore, is needed to ensure adequate governance of the firm. This perspective is reflected in certain definitions which consider responsibilities related to

Finance and Law Perspectives
Corporate governance "deals with the ways in which suppliers of finance to corporations assure themselves of getting a return on their investment" (Shleifer & Vishny, 1997, p. 737)

Management Perspectives
Corporate governance is the set of "formal structures, informal structures, and processes that exist in oversight roles and responsibilities in the corporate context" (Hambrick, Werder, & Zajac, 2008, p. 381) and as "the determination of the broad uses to which organizational resources will be deployed and the resolution of conflicts among the myriad participants in organizations" (Daily, Dalton, & Cannella, 2003, p. 371).

Sociology Perspectives
Corporate governance is the "structure of rights and responsibilities among the parties with a stake in the firm" (Aoki, 2001, p. 11)

Figure 2.1 Definitions of Corporate Governance from differing perspectives.

good governance to be controlling and monitoring management's self-interested behavior. In this sense, governance "*deals with the ways in which suppliers of finance to corporations assure themselves of getting a return on their investment*" since management has been entrusted with the financial investment of shareholders.[3] This definition is more narrow in scope and is typically used by the law and finance professions.[4]

The managerial perspective generally views the board – along with other constituencies – as a resource such that effective corporate governance utilizes these resources in a way that provides the company with a competitive advantage. Under this view, corporate governance is defined as "*the determination of the broad uses to which organizational resources will be deployed and the resolution of conflicts among the myriad participants in organizations*"[5] and refers to a set of formal structures, informal structures and processes that exist in oversight roles and responsibilities in the corporate context.[6] In this way, the board's role can be seen as collaboration and mentoring of top management and aiding them in the formation and implementation of strategy.[7]

The sociological view emphasizes the allocation of power and control among firm participants. From this broader stakeholder perspective, governance is described as the "*structure of rights and responsibilities among the parties with a stake in the firm*".[8] It views the purpose of corporate governance as ensuring that executives respect the rights and interests of all company stakeholders, as well as guarantee that stakeholders act responsibly with regard to the generation, protection, and distribution of wealth invested in the firm.

In sum, a predominant feature of defining corporate governance is to refer to it as a set of constraints, or the general oversight of the firm's structures. In doing so, there exists no definition that connects back to the firm's espoused values. Of course, values are different from other terms discussed in the boardroom like "firm value" and "maximizing share value". As discussed in Part 1 of Chapter 1, moral values are personal and deeply held beliefs about good and bad behavior, desirable and undesirable actions, right versus wrong. Yet, as most of us know, boards also deal with these types of values – from either the firm or the stakeholders' perspective – on a near daily basis. As discussed above, board work is inherently value-laden. Therefore, it's helpful to briefly discuss the stakeholder concept and how that relates to the shareholders of the firm.

Stakes and stakeholders

To understand the concept of a *stakeholder*, it helps to start with its root – a stake. A *stake* is a kind of interest in or claim on something of value. For example, a person or a group who is affected by a certain decision has an interest in that decision. A *claim* could be a legal claim or a right to be treated in a certain way, or even a formal request.[9]

The term stakeholder was coined by the Stanford Research Institute in the early 1960s but later, two academic scholars – Edward Freeman and David Reed – proposed a *broad* definition of stakeholder as "any identifiable group or individual who can affect the achievement of an organization's objectives or who is affected by the achievement of an organization's objectives". They contrast this definition with a *narrow* definition of stakeholder as "any identifiable group or individual on which the organization is dependent for its continued survival". According to Black's Law Dictionary, a stakeholder is "[s]omeone who has an interest or concern in a business or enterprise, though not necessarily as an owner", or (more generally) "[a] person who has an interest or concern (not necessarily financial) in the success or failure of an organization, system, plan, or strategy, or who is affected by a course of action".[10]

While the broad sense definition reveals the perception that multiple and varied groups affect and are affected by the firm (i.e., the *stakeholder perspective*), the narrow sense definition can lead to interpretations that *shareholders*, as a stakeholder group, deserve primacy because they are the foundation of a firm's survival. Shareholders are directly relevant to the firm's core economic interest, which represents the *shareholder perspective*. It's important to note that shareholders are also stakeholders.

While stakeholder can be any identifiable group or individual – from public interest groups, protest groups, government agencies, trade associations, competitors, unions, employees, customers to shareholders – they have increasingly been divided into two categories based on their perceived economic contribution to the firm.

They are sometimes thought of as primary and secondary but have increasingly been categorized as market-based and non-market based with the following characteristics:

- Market – these stakeholders engage in direct economic transactions with the company as it carries out its primary purpose.
- Non-market – these stakeholders do not engage in direct economic exchange with the company but can affect it or be affected by it.

In practice, these terms are often inter-related. For example, companies have changed the focus of their annual 10-K report. In the past, the report consisted of regulatory and shareholder-focused information because annual reports are required by a regulatory body in most countries across the globe, but attitudes about these reports are changing. Now, most of them are glossy stakeholder-oriented brochures that serve a broader purpose. This type of inter-relatedness has become a core element of the ever-expanding duties of the board.

Duties of the board

Indeed, the duties of the board are not only varied but changing with increasing frequency. The 2019 BDO survey of board directors describes it this way:

> *Faced with a deluge of competing and often volatile priorities, public company board directors' oversight responsibilities have reached new heights. Sustaining long-term value today means responding diligently to geopolitical tensions, unrelenting technology disruption, changing regulation, pressures to embrace diversity in the boardroom and more.*[11]

Sound familiar? You have no doubt noticed your own director role changing in just the last couple of years in these exact ways. Therefore, it's important for the actions related to giving voice to values to first set out the basic duties of directors.

In practice, corporate governance encompasses a broad range of legal and non-legal principles and although these most directly regulate the relationships among a company's shareholders, board of directors and management, they may also affect multiple stakeholders – including employees, customers, suppliers and creditors to name a few. This is especially true in the United Kingdom, Canada and many other jurisdictions, that is, to act within a broader duty whereby corporations must take into consideration employees, communities and other stakeholders. Some states in the US have adopted multi-constituency statutes to allow, permit or sometimes require, boards of directors to consider other stakeholders' interests, in addition to those of their shareholders[12]. These 32 statutes also define the stakeholder groups by name[13]. In this way, legal scholars – Lynn Stout and Margaret Blair – believe a US board of directors is "not a policeman employed by shareholders, but a neutral umpire for all involved" indicating the existence of a director – not shareholder – primacy model of governance.[14]

That said, it is typical for the board of directors to be elected by shareholders so they can oversee management and guide the direction of the company while senior managers are responsible for the day-to-day operations of the company. These relationships still form the core of corporate governance, especially in the US. Despite the changes in the way corporate governance has been viewed over time – the various perspectives discussed in Figure 2.1 – directors' fundamental legal duties have varied very little from firm to firm and country to country.

The board has the legal authority to supervise the management of the business affairs of the corporation. In doing so, each director is required to act honestly and in good faith with a view to the best interests of the company – known as the director's fiduciary duty or *duty of loyalty*.[15] As part of this duty, the director must make decisions on an independent basis, in good faith, and with an honest belief that the action is in the best interests of the company and its stockholders. Each director also has a *duty of care* – or the requirement to exercise care, diligence and skill that a person in a similar position would reasonably believe is appropriate under similar circumstances.

While it is true these basic duties have remained largely unchanged, the application of these duties, however, has grown tremendously. For example, under the duty of loyalty, directors must disclose personal financial and other interests in any transaction to the board. And, if there is a conflict of interest – for example, an ownership interest in a contract under consideration by the board – then the conflicted director must be recused from all related deliberations and votes. Also, part of the duty of loyalty is the *duty of confidentiality*. Directors are prohibited from using insider information (i.e., proprietary information that is of competitive or commercial value to the corporation, or information about its finances, operations and strategy). It also covers information regarding the board's proceedings and deliberations.[16]

Under the duty of care, directors are required to attend and prepare for board meetings, listen to and pose questions to the corporation's professional experts (i.e., accountants, lawyers, etc.), deliberate with fellow directors and document the decision-making process (i.e., ensure the meeting minutes accurately represent the discussion and the committee decisions/votes are documented).[17] The duty of care has been applied more generally to the notion of *stewardship*, or the responsible management of something, according to the International Corporate Governance Network (ICGN), established in 1995 to promote global standards for governance and stewardship.[18] One of ICGN's stewardship principles, for example, is dedicated to promoting long-term value creation by integrating environmental, social and governance (ESG) factors into investment decision making. Recently, there has been much discussion on each component, with the "S" under increased scrutiny – driven by multiple social movements and crises in 2020 – such that boards need to address human rights, labor issues as well as workplace health and safety.[19]

Courts generally evaluate violations of the duty of care under the business judgment rule. Under this rule, directors are generally not held personally liable for the consequences of a business judgment if they (1) acted in good faith, (2) were reasonably informed, and (3) and acted with the honest belief the action taken was in the best interests of the company. Factors that come into play are, for example, if a director had a proven conflict of interest and it was not disclosed prior. Courts have been known to look through minutes of board meetings and other documents to determine whether the director and/or board were reasonably informed. Still, the courts generally will not second guess the business judgment of the firm's managers when the duty of care has been met.[20]

These two duties often work in tandem. According to former Delaware Supreme Court Justice Leo E. Strine:

> *A corporate board must make a good faith effort to exercise its duty of care. A failure to make that effort constitutes a breach of the duty of loyalty. In short, to satisfy their duty of loyalty, directors must make a good-faith effort to implement an oversight system and then monitor it [at the board level].*[21]

In June 2019, the Delaware Supreme Court issued a decision which represented a turning point in the evolution of director responsibility to ensure whether the management has adopted an adequate compliance infrastructure to address the company's key risks. In the past, liability for such compliance oversight would be imposed only if the board exhibited a "*sustained or systematic failure*" to exercise oversight, such as an "*utter failure to attempt to assure a reasonable information and reporting system*" from management. In the June decision, via the *Marchand vs. Barnhill* case, the Court adopted an arguably more stringent standard: directors must "*make a good faith effort to implement an oversight system and then monitor it*". Under this standard, corporate boards have an affirmative duty to "ask the right questions" of management and may not escape liability even if management does not inform the board about material risks of which management is aware.

This case represents a growing trend toward imposing liability on both companies and their boards for failing to ensure that they have the information, reporting systems, and the proper committees in place to provide strong oversight of key risk and compliance factors specific to their company and industry.

The corporate governance landscape

There has been much discussion over the past two decades—both in boardrooms and in academic research—about how to fix what is broken in the corporate governance of firms. Regulations and other external mandates have come to be seen as the primary path forward; however, these have proven largely insufficient for ensuring improvements in accountability, transparency, or ethical decision making. Despite ongoing shortcomings in governance practice and mounting public misgivings, attempts to fix what might be broken remains rooted a belief that the solution is structural – that is, if only we could create better rules about how the board is organized, it would function better – and not other factors such as board dynamics, values, relationships and decision-making abilities.

In fact, the governance reform movement over the past two decades is deeply embedded in the formal rules and regulations of global stock exchanges (e.g., New York Stock Exchange (NYSE), Nasdaq Stock Market, Financial Times Stock Exchange (FTSE) European Stock Exchange (Euronext)) and several recent governance principles (e.g., ICGN and Organization for Economic Cooperation and Development (OECD),[22] Commonsense Principles of Corporate Governance, Investor Stewardship Group (ISG). Most – if not all – of these recommendations are structural. See Figure 2.2.

For example, multinational companies listed on either the Nasdaq or the NYSE – the two largest exchanges in the world in terms of total value[23] – experienced a host of structural changes over the past decade, from requirements for the composition of nominating committees, to the independence of the audit committee, to executive compensation plan disclosures. Likewise, according to the OECD's Principles of Corporate Governance, board member independence requirements (via a law or an exchange) have spread in most jurisdictions. At the same time, an independent nominating committee is strongly recommended in these jurisdictions.[24] ICGN, in 2017, created eight Global Governance Principles focusing on board roles

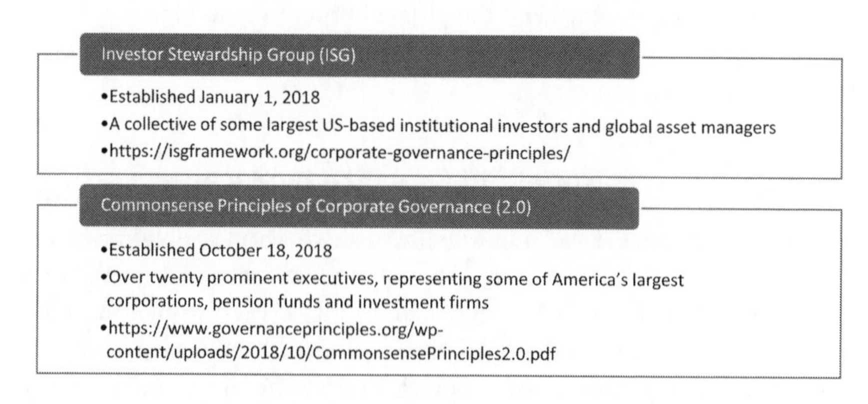

Figure 2.2 Key governance principles (ISG, Common Sense).

and responsibilities, leadership, composition, auditing & reporting, renumeration, risk oversight, shareholder rights as well as corporate culture.[25] Both the Commonsense Principles and the ISG were established in 2018 and both promote equal voting rights, the importance of independent and diverse board members and the need for a long-term focus. Neither discuss stakeholders. Commonsense serves more as a guidebook for various issues like director duties, committee duties and the process for nominating directors. ISG is a set of 6 principles, three of which talk about board structure, inscribing what boards should do. Principle 1 states, simply, boards are accountable to shareholders. Even while these changes have occurred, the public criticisms of corporate governance continue unabated.

Despite these troubling realities, recent global crises also suggest the board has emerged as even more central and influential, comprised of a unique and important set of individuals responsible for providing strategic advice to management and being accountable to shareholders for the actions made by management – in addition to monitoring them.

In fact, in August 2019, the Business Roundtable, a group of large company CEOs and a powerful voice in Washington for US business interests, called for a new purpose for corporations – to view each stakeholder as essential and deliver value for all of them – which departs from its former statement of purpose that focused on an obligation to provide value for shareholders alone.[26] However, as of December 2019, none of the 20 companies – whose CEOs sit on the Business Roundtable's board of directors – had amended their company's corporate governance guidelines to incorporate stakeholder welfare.[27] It should be noted that not everyone agrees with the Business Roundtable – the Council of Institutional Investors responded immediately with the following: "*...we respectfully disagree with the statement issued by the BRT earlier today. The BRT statement suggests corporate obligations to a variety of stakeholders, placing shareholders last, and referencing shareholders simply as providers of capital rather than as owners*".[28]

Although accountability has received some attention in boardrooms, the predominant way of defining corporate governance is by depicting it as either a set of constraints or as the general oversight of firm structures (e.g., standing committees). Certainly, oversight of management is a primary role for boards of directors, but some critics have begun talking about the shortcomings of this structural, agency driven approach for two main reasons: (1) it is void of any ethical decision-making considerations and

(2) it does not address certain personal attributes necessary for individual director and overall board functioning.[29]

Perhaps, it's not surprising then that another primary role of the board has emerged – that of providing access to resources such as advice, knowledge of external events and/or influence with external stakeholders.[30] This role is focused on offering informal advice and counsel, providing strategic input and guiding strategic implementation, strengthening the status and reputation of the firm and gaining access to external resources. What's more is there has been a clear push by the National Association of Corporate Directors (NACD), over the past several years, to underscore that boards have a clear responsibility to exercise oversight of corporate culture because it can be a meaningful corporate asset in a variety of ways (e.g., influencing operational performance, human capital development and organizational reputation).[31]

In turn, according to a 2019 study by the EY Center for Board Matters, boards of directors most commonly rely on management briefings to stay current on megatrends, industry trends, emerging technologies, and potential innovations.[32] Therefore, it's clear the firm's board and its management must form a two-way information exchange.

Let us now delve further into these main roles of the board and its directors with an eye towards the opportunities and challenges these might pose for giving voice to values and what we can do about it.

Notes

1. See Luo, Y. (2005). Corporate governance and accountability in multinational enterprises: Concepts and agenda. *Journal of International Management*, *11*(1), 1–18.
2. The perspective is commonly known as agency theory.
3. See Shleifer, A., & Vishny, R. W. (1997, p. 737). A survey of corporate governance. *Journal of Finance*, *52*(2), 737–783.
4. Aguilera, R. V., Desender, K., Bednar, M. K., & Lee, J. H. (2015). Connecting the dots: Bringing external corporate governance into the corporate governance puzzle. *The Academy of Management Annals*, 9(1), 483–573.
5. Daily, C. M., Dalton, D. R., & Cannella Jr, A. A. (2003, p. 371). Corporate governance: Decades of dialogue and data. *Academy of Management Review*, *28*(3), 371–382.

6. This perspective is associated with what is called behavioral governance. See Hambrick, D. C., Werder, A. V., & Zajac, E. J. (2008). New directions in corporate governance research. *Organization Science*, 19(3), 381–385.
7. Hillman, A. J., & Dalziel, T. (2003). Boards of directors and firm performance: Integrating agency and resource dependence perspectives. *Academy of Management Review*, 28(3), 383–396.
8. Aoki, M. (2001). *Toward a comparative institutional analysis.* Cambridge, MA: MIT Press.
9. The section on stakes and stakeholders is adapted from Clark, C. E., Chang, K. K. & Melvin, S.P. (2020), Business & Society: Ethical, Legal and Digital Environments, 1e. Sage Publications.
10. *Black's Law Dictionary* (11th ed. 2019)
11. BDO Board Survey, The board's direction: Steadying the ship in times of turbulence. See: https://www.bdo.com/insights/assurance/corporate-governance/2019-bdo-board-survey/2019-bdo-board-survey?_cldee=andpdHRAYmRvLmNvbQ%3d%3d&recipientid=contact-a5684d608bbae8118111005056bd67bf-9ca45b232ad540d4a41ec30bf5ca4ba4&utm_source=ClickDimensions&utm_medium=email&utm_campaign=Corporate%20Governance&esid=029daaa5-b3f9-e911-813f-005056bd67bf2019
12. Ronald J. Colombo, Law of Corp. Offs. & Dirs.: Rights, Duties and Liabilities 22:2 (2018).
13. Bebchuk, L. & Tallarita, R. The illusory promise of stakeholder governance. See: https://ssrn.com/abstract=3544978
14. As quoted in S. London, "An Uprising Against Stock Arguments," Financial Times, Tuesday, Aug. 20, 2002. p,10.
15. Please note, a director's duty of loyalty is not the same as the locus of loyalty discussed in the rationalizations section.
16. See Hollinger International, Inc. vs. Black, 844 A.2d 1022 Delaware Chancery 2004.
17. See Hinkley, Allen & Schneider LLP, Aspiring Public Company Director Bootcamp June 6, 2019, Boston, MA. Also Leblanc, R., & Gillies, J. (2005). *Inside the boardroom: How boards really work and the coming revolution in corporate governance*. John Wiley & Sons.
18. See ICGN webpage at: http://icgn.flpbks.com/icgn-global-stewardship-principles/#p=5

19. Fitzpatrick, G. Neilan, J. & Reilly, P. 2020. Time to rethink the S in ESG. See: https://corpgov.law.harvard.edu/2020/06/28/time-to-rethink-the-s-in-esg/#more-130555
20. See https://www.law.cornell.edu/wex/duty_of_care
21. See In re *Caremark International Inc. Derivative Litigation*, Court of Chancery of Delaware, 1996. The Delaware Court of Chancery is widely recognized as the nation's preeminent forum for the determination of disputes involving the internal affairs of the thousands upon thousands of Delaware corporations and other business entities through which a vast amount of the world's commercial affairs is conducted. Its unique competence in and exposure to issues of business law are unmatched. See https://courts.delaware.gov/chancery/
22. OECD is an organization working in partnership with governments, policy makers and citizens in 37 countries to establish international norms. Its principles can be accessed here: http://www.oecd.org/corporate/principles-corporate-governance/
23. Desjardins, J. (2016). All of the World's Stock Exchanges by size. See: http://money.visualcapitalist.com/all-of-the-worlds-stock-exchanges-by-size/
24. OECD (2012), Board Member Nomination and Election. See: http://dx.doi.org/10.1787/9789264179356-en
25. For full list of ICGN principles, see http://icgn.flpbks.com/icgn-global-governance-principles-2017/#p=17
26. For the full Business Roundtable statement, see https://www.businessroundtable.org/business-roundtable-redefines-the-purpose-of-a-corporation-to-promote-an-economy-that-serves-all-americans. Some have argued this "stakeholderism" should considered cautiously, even by those who care deeply about the welfare of stakeholders, due to the current lack of incentives to treat stakeholder interests as an independent end. See Bebchuk, L & Tallarita, R. The illusory promise of stakeholder governance. Electronic copy available at: https://ssrn.com/abstract=3544978.
27. See Bebchuk, L & Tallarita, R. 2019
28. For more information, see CII response at: https://www.cii.org/aug19_brt_response
29. See Bower, J. L., & Paine, L. S. (2017). The error at the heart of corporate leadership. *Harvard Business Review, 95*(3), 50–60 and Filatotchev, I., & Nakajima, C. (2014). Corporate governance, responsible managerial

behavior, and corporate social responsibility: Organizational efficiency versus organizational legitimacy? *The Academy of Management Perspectives, 28*(3), 289–306.

30. See Boivie, S., Bednar, M. K., Aguilera, R. V., & Andrus, J. L. (2016). Are boards designed to fail? The implausibility of effective board monitoring. *The Academy of Management Annals,* 10(1), 319–407.
31. NACD (2017). Core Report of the NACD Blue Ribbon Commission on Culture as a Corporate Asset. See:https://www.nacdonline.org/insights/publications.cfm?ItemNumber=48256
32. See https://assets.ey.com/content/dam/ey-sites/ey-com/en_us/topics/cbm/ey-how-boards-are-governing-disruptive-technology.pdf

PART 3

KEY ISSUES IN THE BOARDROOM

3

MONITORING AND STRATEGY ROLES

To many, the primary role of a board lies in the effectiveness of its ability to protect shareholder interests by hiring the right managers, compensating them properly and overseeing managerial decisions. In fact, most academic research, popular press accounts and government regulation, all echo the deeply held belief that boards should be able to actively monitor management.

One of two approaches is generally offered as the way to achieve this effective monitoring:

1. The first and primary assumption rests on the idea that independent directors can effectively monitor executives.[1] This assumption is so prevalent that, for some, it defines the very meaning of good governance.[2] Independence as a director attribute has largely proliferated because of regulation. Boards of firms listed on a US exchange are required to have independent directors on the audit committee and a majority overall. The 2002 Sarbanes Oxley Act also increased the monitoring role of boards. And – as of 2016 – most member states of the European Union and virtually all major Asian jurisdictions have rules for appointing at least some independent directors to their companies' boards.[3]

2. Second, some believe effective governance can be achieved by hiring board members with the right qualifications – those who bring human and social capital – because they provide these much-needed resources and thus they will use them to monitor management. In this way, the board serves as a provider of resources (e.g., expertise, status, advice and counsel), which are then used to evaluate management.[4]

Bringing an independent director (sometimes referred to as a non-executive director or outside director) to the board is one of the most common value challenges in the field of corporate governance. But, why?

While it may be obvious that independence is necessary for effective monitoring, it is far more complex than that. One of the primary tensions all boards in all countries face is the dual nature of the board's tasks; on the one hand, a board must monitor upper management and on the other, it must provide support for them.

In assessing a director's independence, the nominating and corporate governance committee (i.e., Nom/Gov) needs to take into account certain facts and circumstances. First, it must determine if a director is indeed independent. A director is considered independent when he or she is free from any "material" relationships with either the listed company or with senior management (e.g., commercial, industrial, banking, consulting, legal, accounting, charitable and familial relationships) during the past three years. Second, even if a director satisfies each listed requirement, the board still needs to determine whether the director could exercise independent judgment given the director's specific situation. The NYSE – as well as the Nasdaq – require the board of any listed company to make an affirmative determination of each director's independence, which must be disclosed publicly.

A recent case is illustrative. In 2015, the Delaware Supreme Court in the US ruled that friendship and business relations are together enough to challenge a director's independence.[5] In *Delaware County Employees Retirement Fund v. Sanchez*, No. 702, 2014, 2015 Del. LEXIS 472 (Del. Oct. 2, 2015) (en banc), the Supreme Court held that the long-standing friendships among directors permitted the court to infer that a particular transaction was not approved by a majority of disinterested and independent directors. More specifically, the Court held the audit committee member's personal and business relationships with the chairman of the board inferred that the audit member was not independent from the chairman. When taken in conjunction with the chairman and president's status as interested directors, it meant that a majority of the five-member board was not disinterested and independent when approving the transaction.

In contrast, ownership of a significant amount of stock, or affiliation with a major shareholder, in and of itself, does not necessarily preclude a board from determining that an individual is independent.[6] But, even if a director satisfies each listed requirement, the board must still decide whether the director's independence has been compromised in some way.[7] These examples illustrate some of the board's challenges in classifying independence and whether or not a specific personal relationship is material.

It's likely no surprise there has been some pushback for independence being the solution to what ails corporate governance. Some believe independence can come at the expense of expertise.[8] More strongly, according to Professor J. Robert Brown Jr., it is a myth that directors are chosen primarily on the basis of their qualifications. Instead, he asserts, they are chosen due to their predisposition towards the policies of management.

Another problem is rather obvious – if a director is truly independent then s/he typically has few other sources of information internal to the company other than the CEO or the other board members. And – in order to monitor management – a director must have information about the inner workings of the company. Certain barriers can exist that ultimately inhibit directors from providing effective oversight on an ongoing basis. Chief among these barriers is the board member's ability to obtain, process and act on information from management on a timely basis.[9] At the same time, boards have a duty to "ask the right questions" of management and may not escape liability even if management does not inform the board, as noted above.

Board challenge #1: independence and the gray director

Prized Possession Inc. (PPI) is a mid-cap clothing company listed on the NYSE, primarily targeting women, with a close-knit culture among its executives and top management talent.[10] Its off-beat bohemian style is very popular among women of all age groups and its financial performance has typically been strong since its start in the 1990s. However, at the last board meeting in July, the discussion centered around its declining revenue and what might be the cause(s). PPI's board as a whole has an average tenure of 13 years and is comprised of a total of 9 members, 4 of whom are insiders who work at PPI.

Teresa Hughes, an independent board member for the past 5 years, has observed a troubling trend at PPI – the graying of its directors. *Gray directors* are those who lack perceived independence for one or more reasons but are nonetheless independent for regulatory purposes. Some of these reasons include a director who: serves on a 2nd or 3rd board with another director or the CEO, is a former employee or consultant, receives above market director fees, has social relationships with management or other directors, has an office at the headquarters and uses its administrative staff, or has excessive tenure on one board.[11]

Over time, two of PPI's five independent directors have begun to exhibit what Teresa thinks of as lacking "independence of mind". They do not speak up or question the CEO and founder Dirk Smith, as they once did, and they rely heavily on management briefings to tell them what is going on inside the firm. These two board members have the longest tenure on the board – over 10 years each – one attended college with the CEO in the mid-1980s and the other frequents the same country club as the CEO.

Teresa is not the only one concerned. A large investor group is urging shareholders to vote against the re-election of these two directors, saying the board's "extreme chubbiness" has contributed to its recent weak performance. At PPI's next board meeting, in October, a senior vice president for retail sales is coming to give a management briefing to the board's audit committee about the weak performance.

After thinking about it for a few days, Teresa decided to raise her concerns with the board about the lack of independence and the information barriers at the firm. There is some time before the October board meeting to prepare her approach and work on gaining allies and do some additional data gathering. How does Teresa act on what she knows is the right thing to do?

Applying GVV

Following these three aspects of the GVV framework, we will address them one by one:

- What's at *stake* for the key parties, including those who disagree with Teresa? How can she find *allies* among those who may agree with her? (Inside the board? Outside the board?)

- What are the main arguments she is trying to counter? That is, what are the *reasons and rationalizations* need to be addressed?
- What is Teresa's *most powerful and persuasive response* to the reasons and rationalizations needing to be addressed? To whom should the argument be made? When and in what context?

(1) What is at stake for the parties involved?

Certainly, Teresa Hughes herself has a great deal at stake in voicing her values. Often, people think first of what they, themselves, have at stake. Teresa may be thinking she could lose her directorship or have to face resigning or ill feelings from her colleagues. Given her observation about the graying of some directors, Teresa is aware of each director's own requirement to uphold both the duty of loyalty and care, both of which she must do as well.

And, there's a good chance another director is seeing the graying of the directors and related issues (i.e., there are 2 out of 5 who are perceived as gray). She could find allies within the board, namely, the other 2 non-gray directors. Or, she could also find help from outside of it through the use of a variety of governance professional associations (National Association of Corporate Directors, Society for Governance Professionals, International Corporate Governance Network) or useful data about tenure limits and independence from reports by firms such as EY, PWC, Spencer Stuart, etc.

In this way, and more broadly, the effectiveness of the corporate governance of firms is also at stake in that another example of suboptimal board work is not good for the whole. Therefore, the rest of the PPI board has a great deal at stake. Its ability to make an informed decision, due to the information barriers presented by the clubby relationships, is compromised. This culture may lead to a lack of true dialogue and deliberation and the lack of independence of mind and may be a large contributor to poor decision making and poor performance. Likewise, at stake for some of the current board members is that their board seat is in jeopardy because they could perceive Teresa's comment as suggesting that.

Investors in PPI also have a stake in these outcomes as they invest in companies they believe will perform well. As it stands, investors have already weighed in on their dissatisfaction with PPI's board. Other stakeholders – like employees, consumers and the community – will be impacted by PPI's corporate governance as well.

(2) *What are the reasons and rationalizations Teresa Hughes needs to address?*

Teresa needs to consider at least two key issues – first is these two gray directors may feel threatened if she doesn't approach this situation in a way that is respectful of them. Second, she needs to simultaneously consider whether these directors are, in some way, benefitting from their compromised independence. To be sure, these directors are being paid to monitor management, but at least a few of the directors may argue that all directors in public companies are compromised, at least on some level. After all, it is up to the board to determine whether a director could exercise independent judgment given the facts and circumstances. In this way, they would be using a common rationalization called "standard practice". The statement implies that the directors' eroding independence is acceptable simply because others do it. And yet, since there is no correlation between the ethical value of an action and the number of people who engage in the action, this is a false assumption. If there was such a correlation, this argument might be used to justify any number of harmful actions by boards or top management for that matter.

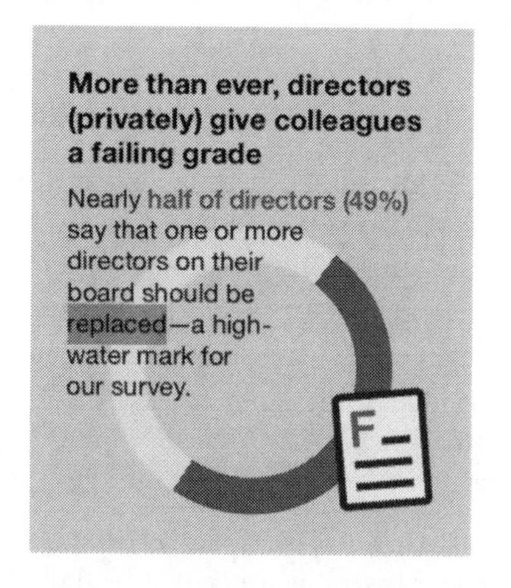

Figure 3.1 Replacing Directors

Source: PwC 2019 Corporate Directors Survey[12]

The rationalization that "everyone does it" can also be addressed through the use of research and/or leading governance practices (e.g., board evaluations). For example, shareholder activists will search director backgrounds for social relationships or other inter-relatedness in order to question a director's independence, and there are new databases from ISS, Glass Lewis, Bloomberg, S&P and other information service providers to increase the ability of activists and others to analyze multiple aspects of a board and individual directors' performance, background and governance standards. Other companies have lost shareholder lawsuits due to intimate personal friendships among board members and/or top management.[13] Similarly, Teresa can refer to the large investor group which is already urging shareholders to vote against the re-election of the two directors, saying the board's "extreme clubbiness" has contributed to its recent weak performance.

Relatedly, Teresa likely faces some directors who rationalize that long-serving directors help capitalize on institutional knowledge and, thus, are a good thing. PPI directors have an average tenure of 13 years, compared with an average of 9.4 years for the S&P mid-cap index, which are companies similar in size to PPI.

Teresa, along with PPI's Nominating Committee, needs to tap into the information readily available about term limits from high profile companies. For example, State Street Global Advisors, the asset management arm of the major financial services firm, embraced a policy in 2014 that takes a skeptical view of boards with average tenure above nine years. Both Blackrock and Vanguard, two of the trillion-dollar institutional investors, followed in 2015 by opposing re-elections of board members of more than 9 years. In July 2017, Microsoft adopted a board tenure policy that avoids the potential adverse effects of an arbitrary bright-line standard, yet is flexible enough to be responsive to investor concerns about board refreshment. The new policy, which is included in its corporate governance guidelines, targets a total board average tenure of ten years or fewer for its independent directors. Perhaps not surprisingly, activist investors campaigning for board seats often argue that long-serving directors have grown too cozy with management. Recently, researchers found the longer the CEO's tenure, the more social ties directors have to the CEO, not unlike those at PPI.[14] Teresa thinks about including some of these facts in her script in an effort to use voice by offering a new way of thinking about a situation and providing additional analyses.

In terms of the director *duty of loyalty*, Teresa Hughes – in voicing her values – is acting honestly and in good faith. Likewise, she is exercising her *duty of care* by employing the diligence and skill that a person in a similar position would reasonably believe is appropriate under similar circumstances.

Teresa also faces a need to talk about lack of information to and from the gray directors. An ongoing issue on boards is the reluctance to speak up when observing either gray directors or watered-down information because there typically exists no protected channel to do so.[15] Teresa must also discuss the responsibility of the board for seeking out unbiased information in order to perform the duties of a director – the "ask the right questions" issue noted above. Often, when the CEO is the founder, it offers these CEOs informational advantages relative to outside directors and in brokering these advantages, it increases their status and power inside the organization.[16]

(3) Practicing the approach and response

Rather than asking what the right thing is to do, Teresa's focus now is on how the board can get the right thing done. Taken together, Teresa reasons she has to take a multi-step approach. First, Teresa believes she could work with her fellow independent board members, in one-on-one meetings or phone calls, prior to the meeting in October to discuss the votes against the two directors by the large institutional investor and how the broader board could handle it. Even though she senses they will be allied with her concerns, she should still be prepared to work through the likely rationalizations just discussed. Her approach, initially, is to create a group of directors, herself included, whose interests and values are aligned.

But, before having a conversation with another director, Teresa should have a good sense of the commonalities among their values and overall goals when compared with hers. For example, do these other board members want to work towards improving the business for the firm (i.e., the ethical value of responsibility), and to work in the interests of the shareholders and likely other stakeholders (i.e., the ethical value of respect), some of whom have become activists. Finally, they all want to feel good about how they represent themselves on the board (i.e., the ethical value of honesty). Perhaps, there are some other shared values? Rooted in these shared values, Teresa is trying to emphasize the alignment and focus on aspirational goals rather than coming off as judgmental.[17] Such a balancing act is not always easy to do.

The backdrop of Teresa's initial conversation is her director duties of loyalty and care. But at this stage, her interest is in teeing up the conversation with her two most likely allies. To do so, she plans to ask them to jointly consider some of these questions as a way to frame the situation –

- "I'd like to hear more about your thoughts around the institutional investor recommendations on these two directors"
- "Could we have a discussion about achieving a mix of tenures in the boardroom? How does our average director tenure benchmark against peers and investor expectations?"
- "How does it compare with the emerging best practices around director independence?" Director tenure?
- "How do we communicate with and manage the conversation so as to be respectful of the 2 directors who are in question here but also meaningfully revisit their independence?"

The second step in Teresa's approach to this challenge is to bring to the forefront the information about these directors' specific circumstances – as these form the basis for their perceived independence. Teresa believes there are three key areas here:

1. the information from the institutional investors' perspective about the 2 directors
2. the personal and long-standing relationships (i.e., 1 college friend and 1 fellow country club member) that the two board members have with the CEO and their subsequent reliance on information from management briefings and
3. the firm's disclosure to the stock exchange about the nature of their independence.

While these three points work together to support the conversation around what is considered independent, the second point is also one that many consider to be a clear sign of a lack of "independence of mind" even though they both may be considered technically independent for regulatory purposes. Thus, has there been a change in perception about these directors' independence and should PPI's public disclosure be revisited?

While ultimately she's building a foundation for their departure, based on data gathering, she believes it's important to create dialogue about these issues so as to convey both a clear sensitivity to her fellow board members and greater transparency to the board as a whole. As a result, Teresa seriously considers starting the dialogue with the whole board by suggesting the board institute director evaluations – after getting buy-in from her two board allies. Conducting evaluations makes good sense because the capabilities and perspectives a board needs evolve over time as the business context inevitably changes. These evaluations allow the board to be critical of itself and focus on an individual director's skill set and performance. With an increased focus on individual director performance by the institutional investor group, evaluations could go a long way in protecting the company against this type of pressure while at the same time ready the board for tenure assessments and substantive refreshment. Teresa is aware such refreshment is often necessary because long-serving board members become too invested in what *is*, rather than what *could* be.[18]

While the outcome of this approach may be the same (i.e., the departure of gray directors), the process is more inclusive of the entire board and if some consensus can be achieved, there is a greater likelihood that the future board's dynamics will not be gravely affected. This reframing away from targeting the two directors is, of course, another way to express voice, that is, by finding another way to accomplish a task that is acceptable ethically. Using this approach may allow the other directors to save face and even participate in the conversation constructively.

(4) Board Exercise

In order to extend the lessons learned with this board challenge, consider Teresa's approach (in whole or in part) and then prepare a script for her – either what she will say to the board as a whole or what she will say when she meets with her two likely allies. Then, have your fellow board members evaluate each other's script draft. Think about the following questions in your evaluation:

- What are its strengths and weaknesses?
- What are the key messages and key arguments?
- How effective do you think she will be?
- How would you improve her approach?

Conclusion

The rules regarding director independence allow for a range of interpretations by the board – and, it is up to the board to determine if a director *could* exercise independent judgment given the facts and circumstances. Part of a director's job, therefore, is to shed some light on issues and policies that are subject to interpretation, and to provide a way to frame the challenge at hand, such as the one Teresa faces with these two gray directors and their personal relationships with the CEO, towards one about preserving the duties of the director and the responsibilities of the firm. In doing so, the conversation and ultimate choice of actions become clearer.

Ultimately, as a director you will need to gauge your own board culture so as to determine whether it's best to alternate approaches and information on a series of decisions where the two gray directors are called upon to see the performance or the perception side of the issue on their own, therefore building a foundation for their departure that is more visible to all. Some boards adopt a simple rule: the truly independent director has the interests of the company and all its stakeholders at heart. Therefore, what course of action will yield the greatest chance of success for all stakeholders in the longer term?[19]

Since a person's independent status can change, another approach is to review the independence of non-executive directors every year. Think of it as an annual "talent inventory".[20] According to Spencer Stuart, two additional initiatives have often proven helpful in hiring for independence – the adoption of fixed terms to reduce the average tenure of directors and innovative measures to increase diversity by drawing from wider candidate pools. Thus, independence is closely related to the director selection process discussed in the next board challenge.

Notes

1. Westphal, J. D., & Fredrickson, J. W. (2001). Who directs strategic change? Director experience, the selection of new CEOs, and change in corporate strategy. *Strategic Management Journal*, 22(12), 1113–1137.
2. Coombes, P., & Watson, M. (2000). Three surveys on corporate governance. *The McKinsey Quarterly*, 74.

3. Harvard Law School Forum on Corporate Governance. See: https://corpgov.law.harvard.edu/2016/08/23/the-rise-of-the-independent-director-a-historical-and-comparative-perspective/
4. Hillman, A. J., & Dalziel, T. (2003). Boards of directors and firm performance: integrating agency and resource dependence perspectives. *Academy of Management Review*, 28(3), 383–396.
5. For more information on *Delaware County Employees Retirement Fund v. Sanchez*, see: https://www.lexology.com/library/detail.aspx?g=22eea24a-4777-489c-b74e-b9ee0442fbd2
6. Commentary to NYSE Listed Company Manual, Rule 303A.02; Nasdaq Listing Rule IM-5605.
7. For more information, see ICGN Governance Principles: http://icgn.flpbks.com/icgn_global_governance_principles/#p=14
8. LeBlanc, R. (2016). Director independence, competency, and behavior. *The Handbook of Board Governance: A Comprehensive Guide for Public, Private, and Not-for-Profit Board Members*, 161.
9. Boivie, S., Bednar, M. K., Aguilera, R. V., & Andrus, J. L. (2016). Are boards designed to fail? The implausibility of effective board monitoring. *The Academy of Management Annals*, 10(1), 319–407.
10. PPI is not a real company, but the board challenge is based on a compilation of actual events.
11. See Fich, E. M., & Shivdasani, A. (2005). The impact of stock-option compensation for outside directors on firm value. *The Journal of Business*, 78(6), 2229–2254. LeBlanc, R. (2016).
12. See PwC Annual Corporate Directors Survey https://www.corporatecomplianceinsights.com/wp-content/uploads/2019/10/PwC-Annual-Corporate-Directors-Survey.pdf
13. See for example the Zynga lawsuit here: https://rroyselaw.com/corporate-securities/entertainment/evaluating-director-independence-zynga-shareholder-derivative-suit/
14. Dey A., Engel E., & Liu X. "CEO and board chair roles: to split or not to split?" *Journal of Corporate Finance* 17/5 (2011): 1595–1618.
15. Leblanc, R. (ed.) *The Handbook of Board Governance*. Wiley Publishing, 2016.
16. Joseph, J., Ocasio, W., & McDonnell, M. (2014). The structural elaboration of board independence: executive power, institutional logics, and the

adoption of CEO-only board structures in U.S. Corporate Governance. *Academy of Management Journal*, 57 (6), See: http://dx.doi.org/10.5465/amj.2012.0253

17. Gentile, M.C. (2010). Giving voice to values: how to speak your mind when you know what's right (p. 28). Ann Arbor, MI: McGraw-Hill Companies, Inc.
18. Refreshment is not the same as replacement of "like for like". See Clark. C. and Brown, J. (2021), "Is Board Refreshment a Ruse of Reality? Available at:
19. See Spencer Stuart Board Composition Boardroom Best Practice https://www.spencerstuart.com/research-and-insight/boardroom-best-practice-chapter-2.
20. Charles Elson comments at the Directors and Boards Virtual Conference Summit, June 3, 2020, https://www.directorsandboards.com/. See also Spencer Stuart Board Composition Boardroom Best Practice.

4

DIRECTOR SELECTION AND THE NOMINATING COMMITTEE

A second topic sometimes marked by values conflicts, and one related to director independence, is the director selection process. The board's process for director selection paves the way for the board's composition and, ultimately, its ability, capability and culture.

In broad terms, *director selection* is defined as the formal or informal process by which individuals are identified and screened for a position on a corporate board. Notably, it is the arena in which the dynamics and the characteristics of the board are established and the overall functionality of the board unfolds.[1] Such decisions are important because the quality of the director appointments is, in part, what determines the board's ability to effectively monitor management and offer strategic advice.

The nominating committee's (NC) main roles are to independently evaluate and nominate perspective candidates for the board of directors and in some cases choose the lead director of the entire board and accept or deny director resignations. Typically, when a potential candidate is identified, an interview process takes place with the board or an executive search firm, if one is used, or by both.

The existence of the NC is important for two reasons: it is responsible for making director selections and appointments and ultimately for the quality of the board - both vital to its effectiveness in terms of monitoring and advising. Ideally, and as intended by various oversight bodies, the NC seeks out potential candidates for board seats independently. The very existence of a nominating committee aims to reduce the influence of the CEO on new director selections. In effect, the members of the NC could have access to more potential candidates from different profiles than the CEO's network, and it allows the separation between management of the firm and control of the firm.

Following governance scandals in the early 2000's and the Sarbanes-Oxley Act, the Securities and Exchange Commission (SEC) made significant inroads to promoting increased transparency regarding the NC and the nomination/selection process. The SEC requires disclosure about the existence and process of this committee and its composition (e.g., level of independence, skills required, and source of nomination).[2] The NC is one of three customary standing committees, along with the audit committee and the compensation committee, required by the NYSE to be composed entirely of independent directors.

Many countries have similar NC requirements.[3] In 2010, under the Dodd-Frank Wall Street Reform Act, the SEC facilitated the nomination of directors by shareholders, further opening up the nomination process to promote shareholder engagement to provide shareholder input into board composition. Despite changes to the NC by various regulatory bodies, the current structure of board selection – in many countries around the globe – consists of a stand-alone NC wherein the CEO has a great deal of influence.[4] To some, the CEO's involvement represents the biggest challenge to true board refreshment, but to others the CEO's recommendation is important because they typically know a lot of people and they need to work with whoever is ultimately selected.[5]

Relatedly, to some, the very idea that director selection is or can be unbiased is misguided. In fact, it has been described as one of the "myths" of board behavior: that the directors of public companies are chosen primarily on the basis of their substantive qualifications.[6] While this may be an extreme view, there are certainly structural and relational elements at play in the nomination and selection process. For example, activist investors campaigning for board seats often argue that long-serving directors have grown too cozy with management. Recently, researchers found the longer the CEO's tenure, the more social ties directors have to the CEO.[7]

In our second board scenario, we return to the case of PPI and Teresa Hughes to look at a board facing a new director nomination.

Board challenge #2: what is our director selection process?

Over the past two years, since Prized Possessions Inc. (PPI) agreed to ask one of its gray directors to resign, who had gone to college with the CEO, shareholders have repeatedly voiced concern regarding what they see as a stale board by filing shareholder proposals that would address the issue.[8] At the recent board meeting, the CEO suggested PPI ask Ms. Audrey Smith to join the board. She has been president of the PPI's most popular brand, *Monterrey*, for the past 15 years. She is PPI's second largest shareholder, outside of her husband, CEO and founder Dirk Smith. The CEO noted her business acumen as well as her ability to bring company-specific and industry-specific knowledge to the board. She would also bring much needed gender diversity to the board. On the board, Audrey will be replacing the SVP of Human Resources who is retiring. Dirk noted that Audrey's retail experience gives her a window into human resource issues.

PPI's NC is a separate committee, staffed by the Lead Director of the board, David Elliott, and two other directors Harry Rubenstein and the Steve Manning who has been on the board for 10 years and frequents the same country club as the CEO. PPI's lead director is an independent, non-executive director. However, it's important to note that while independent board chairs are a common governance practice outside of the US, the practice has been slow to gain ground at S&P 500 companies – only about 1/3 of S&P 500 firms are chaired by an independent director (as defined by NYSE of Nasdaq rules). Presently, just over half (53%) of S&P 500 boards split the chair and CEO roles, up from 35% a decade ago.[9] Typically, however, this change occurs after a crisis or shareholder pressure.[10]

At PPI, Dirk as CEO is often involved in the director selection process either as an informal nominator of the candidate or as an active member of the selection process. While the NC has been part of the process historically, it played a small role compared to the CEO interview with the candidate at the end of the process.

While the CEO does not sit on the NC, he regularly interviews candidates or provides suggestions of people for the committee to interview. He likes to have dinner with the candidate to "seal the deal" as he often remarks. Teresa heard Harry once say, with a nervous laugh, "*We present it*

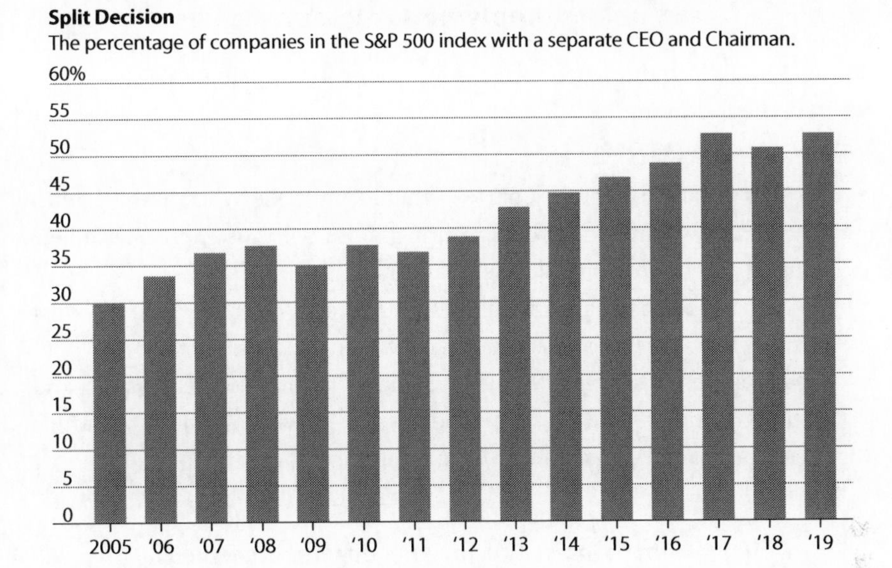

Figure 4.1 Percentage of CEO and Chairman Split.

like this - 'We could do this, or we could do that,' – but Dirk definitely gets to decide." Out of the corner of her eye, she saw a slight wince from David.

The existing nine-member PPI board looks like this:

- CEO (Dirk Smith)
- SVP - HR
- SVP - CIO
- SVP - CFO
- Five independent directors:
  - Steve Manning (frequents same country club as CEO)
  - Teresa Hughes
  - Harry Rubenstein
  - David Elliott (Lead Director)
  - New white male hire from Board Challenge #1[11]

As she reflected over the events of the past few years, Teresa decided to raise her concerns about the PPI director selection process and the staleness of the board's composition. So, she began thinking about the options for her approach.

Applying GVV

Using the GVV framework, place yourself in Teresa Hughes's shoes and address the following:

- What's at *stake* for the key parties, including those who disagree with Teresa? How can she find *allies* among those who may agree with her? (inside the board? outside the board?)
- What are the main arguments is she trying to counter? That is, what are the *reasons and rationalizations* that need to be addressed?
- What is Teresa's *most powerful and persuasive response* to the reasons and rationalizations needing to be addressed? To whom should the argument be made? When and in what context?

(1) What is at stake for the parties involved?

The choice of directors has both important and long-term effects for the board and for the company. It also impacts PPI's other stakeholders, namely its employees, customers, investors and the public at large. Since boards are tasked with holding the company accountable, monitoring its behavior and weighing in on strategy, each individual member has a great deal at stake when directors go about exercising their duties of loyalty and care. Specifically, Teresa Hughes – in voicing her values – has a great deal at stake in trying to instill values such as diversity of thought and gender on the board and yet bringing to the foreground the fact that the candidate is the CEO's wife and, thus, her ability to exercise independence may be compromised. Teresa has her reputation at stake and, potentially, her position as a board member should the CEO view her as challenging his choice. Yet, the CEO has his reputation at stake as well. Is he willing to continue to push the appointment of his wife and, if so, how far? Audrey Smith has a great deal at stake too. While she is a capable manager and brings several other solid qualities to the board, her reputation may be at risk given the perception that her relationship to the CEO could overshadow these accomplishments. Lastly, David Elliott has his role as lead director to think about as he sets the tone for the board and is responsible for the efficacy of the NC.

Ultimately, with this or any other nomination, the three members of the NC (Steve, David and Harry), as well as the board at large, need to consider how stakeholders, including investors, do or would view the diversity of the board and its leadership. Teresa might consider both David and Harry allies given that they appeared to be uncomfortable about the involvement of the CEO in the nomination process for new directors. Teresa knew, from reading recent academic research, that whenever high-level executives (like the CEO) are on the committee or are heavily involved in the director selection process, there may be an incentive on the part of other directors to sugarcoat information when they make presentations or recommendations to the board.[12] Steve, with his country club affiliation, seems to fit this profile.

(2) What are the reasons and rationalizations Teresa needs to address?

First, the rationalizations Teresa will likely encounter undoubtedly stem from the lingering issue of PPI's graying directors. While one of the two graying directors is no longer on the board, the board is still somewhat clubby, white and male. Yet, she senses the board still views the collective institutional knowledge and familiarity as positives overall. And, there are other considerations she must address relating to the broader question of board composition and director selection, which we will deal with following a discussion of the anticipated rationalizations.

Still, the implicit acceptance of the graying of PPIs director independence is very likely a contributing factor to not only the CEO's recommendation that his wife be placed on the board as its second female but also of the willingness for the NC committee to entertain it.

Some board members may rationalize that people who are connected to each other, like some of the board members (i.e., Steve belongs to the same country club as Dirk, and the potential addition of Dirk's wife) is not important to the overall picture – or the common rationalization of materiality. Framing the question in terms of materiality shifts the focus from the action to its consequences and it also minimizes those consequences. Using this rationalization, Teresa is likely to hear directors saying it's not that important to the overall picture. For example, "Audrey is just one director" or "they don't really see each other at the club much". Certainly, however, whether Audrey is or is not a good board choice puts her in an awkward and conflicting position.

In working through these rationalizations, Teresa realizes she should focus on a number of connections being made by the wider corporate governance community. One is that board and committee composition lie at the heart of board decision-making and effectiveness. So, in reality, each and every director selection is very important to the overall picture. Another is that a single director has the ability to alter the board dynamics and culture in a material way.[13] So, it bears considering, at a minimum, how the onboarding of the CEO's wife will affect the current board culture. The trillion-dollar institutional investor, State Street Global Advisors, argues board and corporate culture is a growing intangible value driver that affects a company's ability to execute its long-term strategy. Culture has also been the focus of a recent NACD Blue Ribbon Commission Report and the Financial Reporting Council, noting the board's values drive the culture.[14]

The rationalization of standard practice is one that will come up frequently in the boardroom. In terms of the NC, most of the standards relevant to this committee are found in the applicable stock exchange listing standards. The SEC requires disclosure about the existence and process of this committee and its composition (e.g., level of independence, skills required, and source of nomination), and both Teresa (and her fellow directors) have a fiduciary duty to act in the best interests of investors, and increasingly the broader stakeholder group *(note: see the statement in Chapter 2 as to a firm's broader purpose by the Business Roundtable)*.

As for the stock exchange listings, according to the OECD, most countries recommend the establishment of an independent NC. In both the Nasdaq and NYSE rules – the largest exchanges globally by trading volume – the NC is a requirement and it must be comprised of all independent directors and as for the board as a whole – independent directors must comprise a majority of the board.[15] Thus, in the case of Audrey Smith, she can legally sit on the board as long as she is not on the NC and her being on the board does not shift the majority status of the independence of the board. Still, the question of whether Audrey *can* exercise independent judgment is central to her candidacy and the discussion of it would typically start with the board's lead director, David Elliott, as he presides over the board agenda and sets the tone of the board as a whole. He also sits on the NC.

A third customary rationalization involves one's locus of responsibility. It refers to our sense of who we think bears the responsibility to act in a given situation or who is requiring us to act in a situation. Teresa should expect that other directors may use this rationalization in order to reduce their personal accountability, or that their actions result from the CEO who has the control. It may be the case, then, that Teresa hears some directors claiming they are not the appropriate person to handle the situation, or do not possess the requisite authority to remedy the issue or are simply following directions. Yet, Teresa is aware that her director's duty of loyalty obligates her to act independently, especially of the CEO and his interests. Under this duty, each director is required to act honestly and in good faith while considering the interests of the company. Relatedly, acting in good faith requires that directors take action as opposed to turning a blind eye.[16] Each director also has a duty of care – or the requirement to exercise the care, diligence and skill – that a person in a similar position would reasonably believe is appropriate under similar circumstances.

Fourth, directors can justify their actions using the locus of loyalty rationalization. As noted above, loyalties can conflict. This rationalization can be very effective because it assumes that loyalty to one group necessarily means disloyalty to another group. This may, in fact, be the case with Audrey and although she very likely has the intellectual confidence to think for herself, regardless of her marriage to the CEO, much of the spirit of the independence of directors involves directors not having a relationship with another director or with the company that would impair their independent thought. Still, the moral value of loyalty does not mean doing anything the company wants us to do. It's important to reframe this false "loyalty versus integrity" challenge. For example, a director can acknowledge that being loyal to their colleagues occurs when they stand up to them in voicing their values and beliefs. In this way, we can also define the moral value of loyalty as being transparent with colleagues about our obligations and principles as board members.

It is likely that with any of these rationalizations, Teresa would become more concerned feeling that her own integrity and reputation were on the line because she's increasingly convinced that the status quo would not serve the shareholders to whom she owes a director's duty of care and fiduciary responsibility.

(3) Practicing the approach and prescripting the response

In working through this, Teresa believes there are two core issues: (1) the CEO's involvement in the director selection process and (2) the lack of diversity on the PPI board. Audrey's viability is, perhaps, only a secondary issue to these two. Culling the information from the previous section, it's clear to Teresa that she needs to work with other board members, in one-on-one meetings or phone calls, prior to the next meeting to discuss Audrey's nomination. She could start with the directors on the NC and perhaps start with David Elliott, whom she senses is her strongest ally having seen him express discomfort at an off-hand comment from Harry about the CEO's oversight role in the director selection process. A good first step, in testing his allyship, is to see whether David is seeing what Teresa is seeing, perhaps via a private conversation prior to the full board meeting.[17]

Another related approach would be to contact Harry, the other director with whom she worked on the gray director issue (see Board Challenge #1). She knows Harry is at least somewhat uncomfortable with the CEO's involvement, judging by his quote above. Teresa also knows the three of them were able to help the board to see that one of the gray directors resigning would help dissipate the pressure from the institutional investor group which had expressed interest in voting against him.[18] However, Steve, with his country club affiliation with Dirk (and presumably Audrey), is a tough one to gauge. But, given he is on the NC, they all must consider his position.

But, before having a conversation with Steve, Teresa should have a good sense of the commonalities among their values and overall goals when compared with hers. For example, Teresa might agree that Audrey is qualified to serve on lots of boards. However, for her to sit on PPI's board may not silence the board's critics given that she has a clear conflict being married to the CEO and is not as able to exercise independent judgment for that reason and because she is a company insider serving the president of the Monterrey brand. When discussing this with Steve, Teresa is laying the foundation for a discussion about how he is able to exercise independent judgment.

Teresa also believes she needs to discuss the existing shareholder perception of the board's clubby nature and begin a dialogue about how this does or does not work towards improving the business for the firm (i.e., the ethical value of responsibility), which is presumably a shared value. Speaking about it as a perception will help the other board members understand the concern even if some of them don't agree about the negative impact of this clubbiness. Good governance practices – from multiple professional associations – suggest an additional insider is not ideal for both the oversight of the company and the required disclosure of the nomination (e.g., level of independence and source of nomination). While Audrey may enhance the gender diversity of the board, she will do little to assuage the concerns of the perceived clubbiness. Likewise, Teresa could give voice to the idea that Audrey may, in fact, be put in the position of being a less effective director due to her difficulty in bringing unbiased information to the board, given her marriage to the CEO. If the board still decides to place her on the board, would the board then be setting her up to fail?

In addition to using some of the information from the reasons and rationalizations section, Teresa could script a discussion that broadens the conversation, and effectively moves it away from Audrey specifically. Teresa, in doing so, would be offering a new way of thinking about a situation and providing additional analyses – also an effective use of voice. For starters, Teresa could move the conversation towards a discussion of how much value is being placed on the composition of the board – perhaps noting that many boards today view their composition as a strategic asset and annually review their makeup in light of company strategies and competencies.

Next, she can talk about what disclosing PPIs composition and nomination process would look like and how it might be perceived by important constituents (e.g., investors and regulators). In this way, Teresa is voicing the ethical value of respect by suggesting the board works in the interests of the shareholders and likely other stakeholders. Increasingly, NCs create a board skills matrix to examine the demographics and professional backgrounds of current board members and evaluate the board's composition. Beyond her skills, Teresa could tee up a discussion about how the board is evaluating Audrey's perceived ability to exercise independent judgment. And, in effect, try to gauge how much compromising of a director's independence the PPI board is willing to accept. Relatedly, how will the board disclose its nominating process to the SEC when it did not take into consideration other candidates? This way, she can see where the different perspectives of her fellow board members might lie.

Third, she can talk about diversity more generally and thereby engage ethical values such as compassion, respect and responsibility. The PPI board has a lack of diversity of all kinds – from a perceived lack of diversity of thought (given its clubby perception) and from the standpoint of underrepresented identity groups like females or minorities.[19] With regard to gender, Teresa has a real intractable issue on her hands – having only one woman on the board is problematic for at least two reasons. First, appointing one female director has been criticized for representing tokenism instead of a sincere attempt to increase diversity within the boardroom. Second, studies have shown that many of the benefits of a more gender diverse board are realized only when female directors move beyond a single female.[20] Thus, the case for adding Audrey has positive and negative aspects to it, which forms the basis of conversation it its own right. Here, enlisting Harry and David as male allies is essential so that Teresa does not risk this being relegated to a female problem brought forth by a female.

To this end, the Board Accountability Project 3.0 urges greater diversity among companies' current boards and CEOs. It requests that director searches include non-traditional candidates (e.g., government, academia, non-profits) to broaden the candidate pool.[21] Thus, Teresa can reframe the issue to be one of the need to conduct a robust search process, which, in the case of the CEO recommending his wife, no search process at all was used. Employing a search firm is the dominant form among S&P 500 firm and 73% of FTSE 100% and 60% of FTSE 250 use search firms.[22] It is much less common among small and mid-cap firms.

Similarly, Teresa can enlist the NC (i.e., David and Harry especially) to speak to the issue of separating the CEO from the work of the committee. Here, Teresa can set this up so that she is one of many voices on the issue. Boards are often in this position of needing a process to address the undue influence of the CEO in the nomination process. With PPI, to some degree, this is a separate issue from the fact that the CEO's wife is involved. One way to start is to work towards real and meaningful separation between the NC and the CEO. Creating a strong barrier between the two and expanding the committee's oversight are important to this effort, and in keeping with the spirit, if not the letter, of the SEC's requirements for this committee. However, as the NC's duties include general governance oversight and offboarding of stale directors, such a protective barrier is essential for the delicate tasks of this increasingly important committee.[23]

As part of a conversation with the members of the NC, Teresa plans to work in some of these questions as a way to reframe the situation –

- What is the intended role of the NC per the exchanges and the SEC? How is PPI's NC working to mirror this? In what ways is it not?
- Does the board, as currently constituted, give the company its best shot at success in supporting the strategy?
- Would additional, or even different, skills significantly enhance the board's ability to do its job?
- Does the NC routinely look ahead to identify boardroom needs and anticipated turnover?
- What is PPI's refreshment strategy and how is it communicated to stakeholders, including investors?
- Is PPIs onboarding program for new directors tailored to individual needs and backgrounds and focused on its board culture?

These questions may in fact offer a decision-tree of sorts for Teresa to move forward with. Initially, it seems clear she needs to be certain of the allyship of Harry and David and potentially Steve. So, she can first meet with them separately in order to know where Steve stands, and once determined, can meet with all three members of the NC or just Harry and David. Next, as a primary value of good governance and compliance, she can then tee up a discussion of using a search firm. If a discussion of a search firm is entertained, then she can bring in the need to cast a wide net and reference the diversity initiatives by the Board Accountability Project, noted above. In this way, she effectively reframes the importance of adding another female as the task at hand rather than the issue of Audrey's viability specifically. In the process, she may assuage the concerns of the shareholder activists.

(4) Board Exercise

In order to extend the lessons learned with this board challenge, consider these exercises and questions at your next board meeting:

- Consider the decision-tree offered above. Is this a good approach, or is there another viable set of actions she can take?

- Create an actual script for Teresa. How would you evaluate your fellow board members script for her? What are its strengths and weaknesses?
- What are the key messages the script is trying to send and what are the key arguments addressed?
- How effective do you think she will be?
- How would you improve her approach and her chances?

Conclusion

The landscape within which the NC operates is changing. It is not uncommon to have an evolving set of pressures from large institutional investors, proxy advisory firms and regulators attempting to weigh in on the board's NC policies and practices.[24] Shareholder resolutions pressing for greater diversity are not unusual either. So, the pressure is mounting for firms like PPI to address the lack of diversity. For example, State Street Global Advisors, in a recent guidance note, stated it will engage directly with those firms it invests in to encourage the addition of more female directors and is prepared to vote against NC chairs of boards that fail to do so – yet another concern for PPI's lead director David Elliott. Proxy advisors are also exerting their considerable influence; in its most recent policy guidelines, Glass Lewis featured more discussion of board gender diversity in its reports, including a phased policy that directly targets nomination committee chairs with "against/withhold" votes if boards do not include a female director, or provide a cogent explanation.

PPI, at a minimum, must take time to consider what its NC policies are – as it appears its selection process with Audrey was more CEO-driven – and be prepared to explain its rationale for these policies. Part of a director's job is to shed some light on these issues and to provide a way to frame the challenge at hand, such as the one Teresa faces with the director selection process.

In fact, the NC, some suggest, should be renamed the governance committee to indicate its growing oversight of shareholder/employee engagement, corporate culture and overall talent management.[25] International company L Brands – seller of lingerie, personal care and beauty products, apparel and accessories – is an illustrative example. In 2019, facing criticism that the marketing of its Victoria's Secret business was no longer aligned with women's evolving views of beauty, diversity, and inclusion, L Brands added more outside female directors to its board with experience in areas including merchandising and marketing in order to offer different perspectives regarding line functions but also of gender identity to better mirror their consumers.[26] This example offers another approach PPI could take as it too is a retailer especially popular among women.

In evaluating board composition, some companies have asked a demographer to speak to the board about the motivations of upcoming younger generations and how best to attract and retain people who are more mission-driven and concerned about the values of the corporation.[27] And, COVID-19-related challenges have ushered in a renewed interest in generalists as board members, especially those who understand board versus management roles in crisis situations, aspects that niche directors typically do not possesses.[28]

In raising some of these values conflicts in director selection and board composition, the conversation and ultimate impact of the board's choice of actions can be broadened to these additional areas of concern.

Notes

1. Clune, R., Hermanson, D. R., Tompkins, J. G., & Ye, Z. (2014). The nominating committee process: a qualitative examination of board independence and formalization. *Contemporary Accounting Research*, 31(3), 748–786.
2. See SEC rules at https://www.sec.gov/rules/final/33-8340.htm
3. Organization for Economic Cooperation and Development (OECD) (2015). G20/OECD Principles of Corporate Governance, Paris, France: OECD Publishing. http://dx.doi.org/10.1787/9789264236882-en
4. Clune, Hermanson, Tompkins, & Ye, 2014
5. Comment made in board interview August 15, 2019.
6. Brown, J. R. (2015). The demythification of the board of directors. *American Business Law Journal*, 52(1), 131–200.
7. Dey, A., Engel, E., and Liu, X. CEO and board chair roles: to split or not to split? *Journal of Corporate Finance* 17/5 (2011): 1595–1618.
8. PPI is not a real company, but the board challenge is based on actual events.
9. See Spencer Stuart Board Index Report 2019, p. 6.
10. Gryta T and Francis, T., (2019, November 3) When things get tough, companies split chairman, CEO roles. Wall Street Journal. See: https://

www.wsj.com/articles/when-things-get-tough-companies-split-chairman-ceo-roles-11572778801?emailToken=7d468d7d438edac745efaa75dbc06c14wDLLGgl/eCvUdm90YEVB05K/G1V/qxig6D18LvpVFFjYdj1Sa+Jbv+DYq7BGFQ4s4XJxCLxmJYF1i3VJxwhng8zt6BP9cVHn9awUTPAOjXhkgg0kN2IAmMbpucJ2Ubzl&reflink=article_email_share

11. This new hire replaced the gray director in Board Challenge #1 who went to college with CEO Dirk Smith.
12. LeBlanc, R. (2016) *The Handbook of Board Governance.*
13. Comment from board interview, October 1, 2019.
14. See https://www.nacdonline.org/insights/blue_ribbon.cfm?ItemNumber=48186. See also https://www.frc.org.uk/getattachment/3851b9c5-92d3-4695-aeb2-87c9052dc8c1/Corporate-Culture-and-the-Role-of-Boards-Report-of-Observations.pdf
15. Both exchanges, more specifically, have minimum definitions for determining director independence and also require boards to affirmatively determine that directors who are classified as independent have no material relationship with the company, either directly or as a partner, shareholder or officer of an organization that has a relationship with the company. See also NYSE sample disclosure form here: https://www.nyse.com/publicdocs/nyse/regulation/nyse/NYSE_Domestic_Company_Initial-Annual_Written_Affirmation_303A.pdf
16. Colombo, R. J., Law of Corp. Offs. & Dirs.: Rights, duties and liabilities 22:2 (2018).
17. Comment from board interview, October 1, 2019.
18. Gray directors are those who lack perceived independence for one or more reasons but are nonetheless independent for regulatory purposes. Some of these reasons include a director who: serves on a 2nd or 3rd board with another director or the CEO, is a former employee or consultant, receives above market director fees, has social relationships with management or other directors, has an office at the headquarters and uses its administrative staff, or has excessive tenure on one board.
19. For an explanation of the difference see Geletkanycz, M., Clark, C. E., & Gabaldon, P. (2018). When boards broaden their definition of diversity, women and people of color lose out. *Harvard Business Review.* Available at: http://d2f5upgbvkx8pz.cloudfront.net/sites/default/files/

inline-files/Research_%20When%20Boards%20Broaden%20Their%20Definition%20of%20Diversity%20Women%20and%20People%20of%20Color%20Lose%20Out%20%28002%29.pdf

20. Guldiken, O., Mallon, M., Fainshmidt, S., Judge, W. & Clark, C. Beyond tokenism: How strategic leaders influence more meaningful gender diversity on boards of directors. *Strategic Management Journal*, 40(12): 20242046.
21. Board Accountability Project 3.0. See: https://comptroller.nyc.gov/newsroom/comptroller-stringer-launches-boardroom-accountability-project-3-0-a-first-in-the-nation-initiative-to-bring-diversity-to-board-and-ceo-recruitment/. The project also calls on companies to adopt a "Rooney Rule" policy, i.e., a policy requiring the consideration of both women and people of color, for every open board seat and CEO position.
22. See Akyol, A. C. and Cohen, L. Who chooses board members. *Advances in Financial Economics*, 16 (2013): 4375. See Doldor, E., Sealy, R., and Vinnicombe, S., Accidental activists: headhunters as marginal diversity actors in institutional change towards more women on boards. *Human Resource Management Journal* 26/3 (2016): 285303; Doldor, E., Vinnicombe, S., Gaughan, M., and Sealy, R., Gender diversity on boards: the appointment process and the role of executive search firms. *Equality and Human Rights Commission Research Report* 85 (2012): 1-98.
23. Goodman, A., The rise and rise of the nominating and governance committee, *Russell Reynolds Associates* (February 27 2020), accessed March 3 2020. See: https://www.russellreynolds.com/newsroom/the-rise-and-rise-of-the-nominating-and-governance-committee
24. Proxy advisory services provide voting recommendations on topics including director elections, shareholder proposals and mergers, and company-specific voting recommendations; proxy advisory services publish voting guidelines setting forth their policies on various issues.
25. For more information, see The Conference Board: https://www.conference-board.org/blog/postdetail.cfm? post=7177&mkt_tok=eyJpIjoiT1RobE5UVmhPR1V5TURWaSIsInQiOiJHazA4Sk1zbnppSnpYZXhVRXJpV3lmZzdoMDFTNnBvRE9oTWtzVTQxQ2k2VW9uOUNoR3poK01WaUc2RnZGV1JCbXJzazJvblBEZWp6UVJoZFByYWFYXC8xMExXVFpBOWdwditXS GNvWXFzbHN5Y

26. Landaw, J. How diverse is your board really? *Harvard Business Review*, June 11, 2020. See: https://hbr.org/2020/06/how-diverse-is-your-board-really
27. Comment made in board interview August 15, 2019.
28. Prince, C.J. 2020. A time when generalists are most needed. *Corporate Board Member*. See: https://boardmember.com/a-time-when-generalists-are-most-needed/

5

CEO SUCCESSION

One of the main features of the board's monitoring functions is ensuring the right management team is in place to run the organization. The SEC agrees. In its Staff Legal Bulletin No. 14E, it stated, "one of the board's key functions is to provide for succession planning so that the company is not adversely affected due to a vacancy in leadership".[1] One of the biggest challenges in this capacity is hiring, evaluating and firing the CEO and succession planning. Given the high turnover and cause-related terminations, the challenge is even greater in today's boardroom.

Consider a few statistics. According to a recent Equilar study, the median tenure for CEOs at large-cap S&P 500 companies was 5 years at the end of 2017.[2] In 2019, for the first time, boards dismissed more CEOs for ethical lapses than for financial performance or conflicts with directors, according to PwC's CEO Success study.[3]

Given the short CEO tenure and the increasing dismissals, these statistics alone suggest CEO succession planning is a must. Adding to the pressure is the SEC's desire to make succession planning an integral part of good corporate governance,[4] but research shows boards are not giving enough importance to the matter.[5] According to NACD's Governance Challenges 2019 report, 56% of public directors report that CEO succession planning is an area where improvements are important or very important over the next 12 months.[6] In environments marked by extreme disruption, like the COVID-19 pandemic, boards must also have an emergency succession plan that can be implemented at a moment's notice.[7]

Another key aspect to consider in CEO succession planning is where the typical successor comes from. Nearly 80% of CEO succession candidates come from inside the organization, according to Equilar's recent Corporate Governance Outlook.[8] For internal candidates, there is often a talent disconnect given that companies tend to do a poor job of cultivating talent. And, according to search firm Spencer Stuart, less than a third of directors have regularly scheduled meetings with the CEO's direct reports – those most likely to be in the line of succession.[9] Governance experts suggest maintaining a regularly updated list of potential successors outside the company as well, especially those with relevant experience for the future direction of the company.[7] Relatedly, for testing CEO candidates, there is a heavy reliance by the board on formal presentations with candidates, arguably not the best way to view someone's ability to navigate the complex and dynamic set of interactions required of a CEO.

Experts suggest starting early – during the present CEO's tenure – helps to make succession planning an ongoing activity and discussion rather than one that signals a problem.[10] Because, as one board advisor put it, too many boards look like absentee landlords rather than hands-on owners when it comes to planning for the future of the firm.[11] In other words, some boards are reluctant to address succession planning, particularly if the current CEO is long serving or the founder of the company. According to Spencer Stuart, "overcoming resistance to raising the issue with the CEO – or, in the most difficult situations, forcing the issue with a reluctant CEO – continues to be a challenge for many boards."[12]

Another related trend affecting CEO succession is the prevalence of retiring CEOs who remain on the board. According to researchers as of 2018, some 35% remain with the company in the role of the chair.[13]

Board challenge #3: CEO succession and planning for the future

Mandar Group is a bank holding company serving several Southern states in the US. It was founded in the 1900s by the Grande family who prides itself on the relationship-based business it created.[14] Javier Grande is the son of the founder and has held the CEO position for 20 years. Mandar's board as a whole has an average tenure of 12 years and is comprised of a total of 10 board members, 1 of which is female.

Traditional banking has undergone great change in the past decade. Technological advancements like cryptocurrency and fintech have put pressure on the Mandar Group to modernize. One of the key challenges for Mandar in the next five years is how to deploy fintech to improve the use and delivery of its financial services. As of December 2018, 40% of the adult population across the globe actively use a digital platform for banking.[15]

Another challenge for Mandar is the lack of trust in the industry as a whole. The 2019 Edelman Trust Barometer, focusing on financial services, indicates trust in the sector is at its highest level since Edelman started measuring it in 2012. But at 57%, trust in financial services, among the general population, remains the least-trusted sector (see Figure 5.1).[16]

The Chief Human Resources Officer (CHRO), Sofia Adams, is a close personal friend of the CEO's wife having attended college together at Texas Tech. Recently, Sofia attended an HR conference and the subject was CEO succession planning. And, although she tried to broach the subject previously, she has been unsuccessful in getting Javier to talk about retirement or succession planning in a meaningful way. She has been successful in getting the board to conduct annual board evaluations about a variety of topics and recently asked about its executive succession planning quality.

Javier, who is 73 years old, has been reluctant to discuss his successor. He is an avid outdoorsman, likes to play golf, and often talks about his low body fat and recent hunting expeditions. He thinks the board likes to hear about these things, and he believes his is a "young" 73. Every time Sofia or the board brings up possible internal candidates, he can't help but think of personal reasons to show why his successors would not be a good fit – one person's husband drinks too much, another is not a nature lover, and another took a nap on their recent plane ride together.

One thing Javier and the board do agree on is the personal focus of the banking industry, but he admits he is not a big fan of fintech. He believes it takes away the personal touch. He's also a bit worried it is not as secure a platform as it purports to be.

One very experienced director, Tomás Blanco, is a former bank CEO and is seeing the classic signs of a reluctant retiree in Javier. He realizes he needs to discuss with Sofia her involvement in the process because, as he sees it,

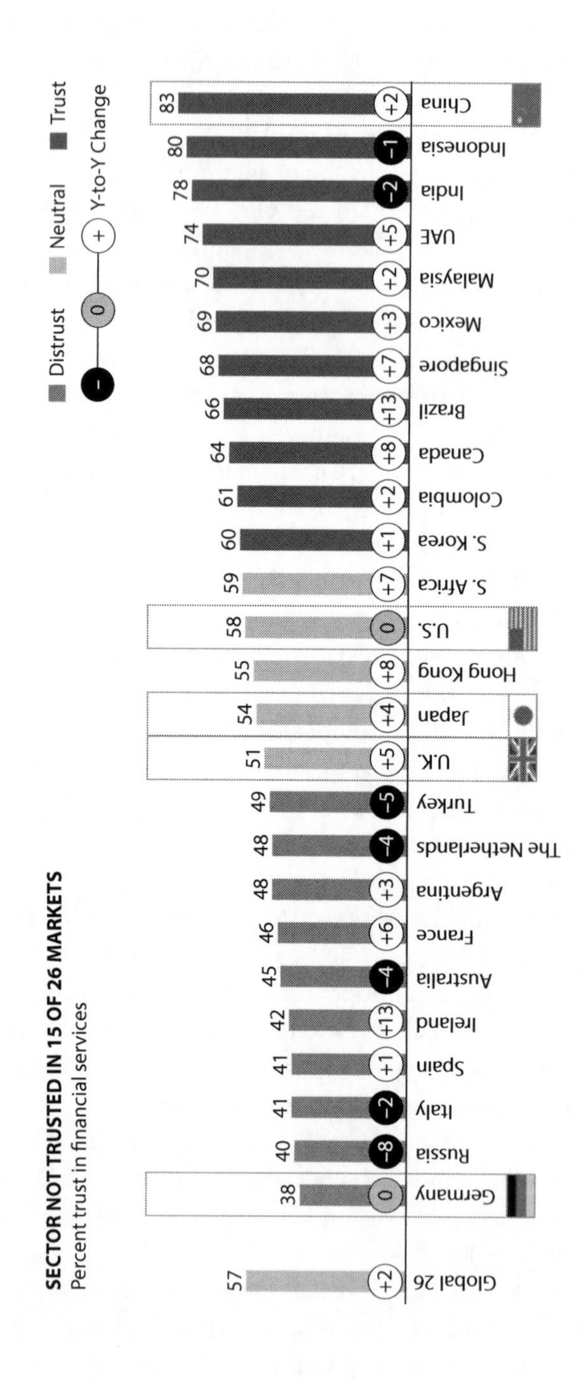

Figure 5.1 Least trusted business sectors.

Source: Adapted from the 2019 Edelman Trust Barometer: Financial Services report

the CHRO is a vital link between the CEO and the board and a potential advocate for best practices. Tomás knew what he needed to do, at a minimum, was to help the board see the benefits of a succession plan. He began thinking about his approach.

Applying GVV

Using the GVV framework, place yourself in Tomás Blanco's shoes and address the following:

- What's at *stake* for the key parties, including those who disagree with Tomás? How can Tomás find *allies* among those who may agree with him? Does anyone agree with him (inside or outside the board)?
- What are the main arguments Tomás is trying to counter? That is, what are the *reasons and rationalizations* he (they) needs to address?
- What is his *most powerful and persuasive response* to the reasons and rationalizations needing to be addressed? To whom should the argument be made?

(1) What is at stake for the parties involved?

To begin with, as is the case in giving voice to values, it is clear that Tomás already knows what the right thing to do is – create an effective succession plan for Mandar. Tomás has a stake in CEO succession as do the shareholders, regulators and consumers of the bank as well as Javier himself. How well, or poorly, the board handles a CEO succession plan can have a direct impact on the company's success. Handled poorly, it can leave a company vulnerable to media attack and shareholder activism. Handled well, it can help the company gain stock value, reputational capital and employee morale. To many, this transition is a marker of how the company manages itself overall. According to the SEC, CEO succession planning raises a significant policy issue regarding the governance of the corporation that transcends the day-to-day business of managing the workforce – and one it feels shareholders should be able to ask about.[17]

His duties as a director – and the decision-making around who leads the Mandar Group into the future – has serious impacts for Tomás and the stakeholders he serves. His duty of care requires him to address major business risks, including the planned or unplanned transition to a new CEO. Simply put, Tomás is required to act in an independent manner with the good faith belief that such actions are in the best interest of Mandar (i.e., the fiduciary duty of loyalty).

With the changes noted in the banking and financial services industry above, a forward-thinking CEO is necessary to provide returns to shareholders and loans and other financial services to consumers. Given the interconnectedness of the global financial system, government regulators also have a great deal at stake in keeping the Mandar Group in good competitive standing among its peers.

Javier also has a great deal at stake. Very often, the company and the founding CEO's identity are intertwined. It would not be unusual for Javier, like many founders, to have difficulty envisioning the bank without himself at the center of it. His comments about other possible replacements make this feeling rather clear. After all, the future success of the bank is also at stake for Javier – both while he is CEO and once he eventually retires.

Likewise, the Nom/Gov and Compensation committees of the board have a stake as they commonly handle CEO transitions. In the same way, Sofia has much at stake because she is – or is not – perceived as a person who can help with this transition, specifically in cultivating the internal candidates (which is typically the first choice of most boards) and creating a development plan for all candidates over time (e.g., filling in gaps they might have through exposure to certain business areas). Yet, both the Nom/Gov and Compensation committees – as well as Tomás himself – could be instrumental in creating a list of external candidate names, but his initial concern is how to get the board to recognize the need for a succession plan.

Tomás would be wise to find *allies* who may agree with him. He believes Sofia, the CHRO, is the best link to the CEO, not only because of the position she holds but her personal relationship as well. Of course, the latter might pose a challenge. Likewise, Tomás – who sits on the audit committee – might find allies among those on either the Nom/Gov or Compensation committees – directors who share the same duties as he does in terms of mitigating future risk. Additionally, since Tomás is a former bank CEO, his network of other CEOs could prove a useful link to outside allies (and possible external CEO candidates) to help him script his eventual talking points to the board. Oddly enough, the financial press might be an ally of his as there are numerous and frequent reports of CEO demise, turnover and refreshment.

(2) What are the reasons and rationalizations Tomás needs to address?

As noted earlier, it's sometimes challenging to talk about our values and immediately change the behaviors of others because, typically, our inner thoughts and emotions routinely present us with a rather sophisticated set of rationalizations for either acting or not.

While there is widespread documentation that boards do not effectively attend to CEO succession planning, despite agreeing on its importance, Tomás needs to be ready for the "standard practice" rationalization. This argument assumes that an action is acceptable simply because the majority of the people engage in it or because it is something that has been done for a long period of time. This rationalization is often used to avoid taking responsibility. It's likely that Javier will take any suggestion of a plan personally, knowing it is not a specific regulatory requirement or standard practice at Mandar.[17] However, both Sofia and Tomás could be advocates for best or leading practices over the more common practice of putting their heads in the sand.

It might come as no surprise that the rationalization of materiality will come up. It refers to making the argument that ultimately planning for Javier's successor in advance doesn't matter because it won't make a difference in the long run, given Javier's reluctance. This rationalization is clever because it frames the question in terms of impact, versus board accountability, and thus shifts the focus from the action to its minimal consequences. While there are board members who are likely to argue this, Tomás should be particularly concerned should he hear it from Sofia in her role as CHRO, especially given her recent attendance at a conference on the subject of CEO succession.

A third concern is the locus of responsibility rationalization. Truth is, CEO succession is everyone's problem. This rationalization usually reduces personal accountability while giving it over to some authority figure who presumably has the control. Sometimes, we hear people claim they are not the appropriate person to handle the situation, or do not possess the authority to remedy the issue. It may, in fact, be something Sofia claims. For example, she might push back on Tomás to make it a board-wide responsibility. While, technically, she may be correct, the board very much depends on the CHRO to guide a thoughtful, orderly and transparent process and ensure that directors have the information they need to make the best decision on the candidate when the time comes. Also, the Nom/ Gov Committee may defer to the Compensation Committee or vice versa, making the ultimate responsibility a finger-pointing exercise that doesn't address the problem of board accountability for the succession plan.

Given both her loyalty to her job and her loyalty to Javier's wife, Sofia is likely to have conflicting loyalties. Tomás needs to carefully consider how her relationship to the CEO's family could be an issue for her and, because he needs to work with her in her CHRO role in succession, an issue for him as well. Sofia may likely offer a rationalization to Tomás that hides where her locus of loyalty lies. He needs to watch out for assuming that loyalty to one group necessarily requires disloyalty to another group. This is a tricky one because it is likely Sofia is wrestling with the conflict between truth and loyalty – both solid values. She may, in fact, want to be honest and transparent about her relationship with the CEO and his wife (i.e., the ethical value of truth) and her loyalty and commitment to the job itself. The real question is whether having a relationship with the CEO's family impairs her independent thought about needing a CEO succession plan, or can Tomás count on Sofia to accommodate both?

(3) Action planning and prescripting the response

In thinking this through, Tomás may want to start with allies that are likely to share his values in relation to the issue at hand. Principally, he needs to probe his fellow directors for their thoughts on how the absence of a succession plan works against improving the business and the best interest of the firm (i.e., the ethical value of responsibility). For example, there is a short-term versus long-term tension here between what might be best for the firm now (i.e., Javier's leadership) and what might be best for its future (i.e., a smooth transition to a more technologically adept CEO). Likewise, he needs to identify which directors most clearly believe the board must work in the interests of the shareholders and likely other stakeholders with regard to CEO succession (i.e., the ethical value of respect). Finally, directors are likely to want to feel good about how they represent themselves on the board (i.e., the ethical value of honesty).

For Tomás, in keeping with his attempt to find allies and shared values, the first step is to get some useful background information. For example, which board committee at Mandar is responsible for succession planning? Once determined, he can make sure it is outlined in the committee charter. Tomás can also check in with his CEO network to get a sense of the best practices and prepare to report this to the appropriate committee. These steps are, in fact, other ways to give voice to a problem.

Tomás also needs speak with Sofia. Here, he begins to craft a decision tree. First, he decides to start by asking some questions about her recent conference takeaways. If Sofia articulates some sort of plan of action she learned, Tomás can pick up on positive elements such as the need to make CEO succession a regular board agenda item, or that it protects Javier's legacy, or that it will likely keep investors from demanding details of the plan, which they can request via a shareholder resolution per the SEC.

Given that Sofia has conducted board evaluations about CEO succession, another part of his action plan is to ask to see the last few evaluations to get a sense of how satisfied directors are with the succession planning process and where they see room for improvement. If he can ally with Sofia and use these evaluations to capture the board's sentiment about CEO succession, then this is a good place to start.

Next, he needs to check in to see where she is on the conversations she's had with Javier, or even his wife (her close friend). He knows she has had some discussions, and they didn't go well, but Tomás doesn't know the particulars of the conversation. This is a delicate situation, but the potential is high for Sofia to play a trustworthy link between the board and the CEO. On the one hand, Sofia may be able to better understand, through her friend, Javier's reluctance about moving on. On the other hand, it may cause tension because Sofia believes her job is conflicting with her personal relationship and prefers not to ask her friend about it. Tomás could offer to help her think through this. In doing so, Tomás needs to pay particular attention to the balance between her ability to provide a link and her potential level of bias. While many of the other directors may develop biases about certain processes or even candidates, the CHRO must be the one who ensures the honesty and integrity of the process, and who makes sure that each executive regularly goes through an assessment. Therefore, a final decision Tomás needs to make is whether Sofia can exercise independent judgment – or whether he needs to bring in other directors – like those on the Nom/Gov or Compensation committee.

However, if Tomás does not find an ally in Sofia, he decides he could then take another approach by beginning a dialog with the Nom/Gov or Compensation committee chair, whichever is responsible for succession planning. He thinks he should start with these three questions:

1. Have we identified the planned retirements of the senior management team within the next 3-5 years? How does this affect potential CEO candidates?
2. Ideally, if we were able to put a transition plan in place, what steps would be needed to make this transition work best? Where do we start?
3. What is the role of the Nom/Gov and Compensation committees in this plan? What is the role of the CHRO in talent management? How should HR and the board work with one another?

Tomás needs to script his discussion to a reframing of the issue as one of oversight of management development, rather than simply preparing for a CEO change.[18] This will help to address the inherent planning challenges and expand the board's understanding of its internal capacity to manage this process or whether it needs to engage an external firm for help in the process. Also, Tomás can speak about the importance of CEO legacy as he, himself, was a bank CEO and because Javier cares about his legacy.

In addition, Tomás believes these three topics are central to any effort to reframe the situation. So, he jots down several notes to himself–

1. *Succession Planning as a Board Agenda Item*: How can we get a discussion of the process of succession planning on the board agenda as a perennial item? Things to consider:
   - We want to avoid the common pitfall of it being a discrete event. How can we broaden the discussion to a board review of specific

threats or opportunities that may affect the company as a central part of the company's strategic planning process?[19]

- Who will take over in the event of Javier falling ill suddenly or being accused of an ethical lapse (e.g., emergency succession plan)? There is also the issue of Javier being CEO far beyond the average tenure.

2. *CEO Succession Planning Roles:* Specific issues on his mind are: how can we, as part of the planning process, outline clear roles? For example, who will take the lead on the search (whether internal or external), what will the outgoing and incoming CEO be paid (see next scenario for executive compensation)? Who will address the SEC and exchange requirements for departure? For when the new CEO is hired?[18]
   - Outline the board's responsibility to hear from and engage with the CEO's direct reports – perhaps via board presentations – so the board can get to know them. Consider broaching the subject of making a list of external candidates.
   - Discuss the need to avoid the common pitfall of having the current CEO on the transition team. Incumbent CEOs have an inherent conflict of interest in identifying and grooming potential successors. Since many CEOs are like Javier, and are not looking to be replaced, the stronger the potential successor pool, the more likely it is for the board to think the CEO is, in fact, not irreplaceable.[20]

3. *Engaging the CEO:* While Tomás is focused on helping the board see the benefits of a succession plan, a key part will eventually also involve thinking through how best to talk about it with Javier.
   - Of concern is how to frame the issue as something Javier will be invested in as opposed to something that feels like a threat. Tomás could stress Javier's awareness of the possibility of shareholders demanding a CEO succession plan (per SEC bulletin information above).
   - Or, reframing it by asking Javier to articulate how the leadership team supports the current and future business strategy. How will fintech change this?
   - And, eventually, the board needs to consider not only who will eventually speak with Javier but also whether he should play a role in the transition, once a succession plan is agreed to.

(4) Board Exercise

In order to extend the lessons learned with this board challenge, consider undertaking this exercise at your next board meeting or retreat:

- Choose one of the three questions for the committee responsible for succession planning, mentioned above, and create a script for Tomás. Or, consider the decision tree with Sofia, and create a script for Tomás. Use any part of the case or the prescripting section.
- Have one of your fellow board members evaluate his script. What are its strengths and weaknesses?
- What are the key messages he is trying to send and what are the key arguments he is trying to address?
- How effective do you think Tomás will be? How can his approach be improved upon?
- Once the action plan and script for Tomás have been settled on, create an action plan to approach Javier.

Conclusion

The landscape within which CEO succession planning operates is always changing. And, although some boards do this planning well, there remain many challenges for boards that can be scripted and prepared for, as outlined in the case of the Mandar Group. Regardless of the specific circumstances of your board, Spencer Stuart suggests that all boards are wise to get started early and revisit the plan regularly, outline the successor criteria and make sure it is forward-looking, and develop a rich succession pipeline in concert with your CHRO.[21]

Or, it might be helpful to take the innovative approach of Novartis CHRO Steven Baert. When the company recognized its culture was no longer fit for the future of the firm, the CEO helped establish a goal to "#unboss" the traditional pyramid hierarchy. He stated in a widely circulated LinkedIn post that "the emerging workforce is looking for a new kind of leadership… They don't want old-fashioned micro-managers or hierarchies: instead they want collaborative, purpose-led leaders who create clarity, serve people, are open to feedback and focused on removing obstacles and empowering their teams." He describes this "unbossing" journey one where firms no longer have a team in support of a boss; you have a boss in support of a team".[22] Might such a discussion be a precursor to a CEO succession plan?

Notes

1. SEC Staff Legal Bulletin 14E, October 27, 2009. See: https://www.sec.gov/interps/legal/cfslb14e.htm
2. Harvard Law School Forum on Corporate Governance. See: https://corpgov.law.harvard.edu/2018/02/12/ceo-tenure-rates/
3. https://www.strategy-business.com/article/Succeeding-the-long-serving-legend-in-the-corner-office?gko=90171
4. The SEC views succession planning as a significant policy issue — so much so as of 2009 it requires boards to entertain shareholder proposals on succession planning.
5. https://insights.diligent.com/ceo-succession/executive-ceo-succession-planning-for-corporate-boards/
6. https://blog.nacdonline.org/posts/new-research-spotlights-ceo-succession-challenges
7. Spencer Stuart, 2020. Now is the time to revisit your emergency succession plan. See: https://www.spencerstuart.com/-/media/2020/april/emergency_succession_plan_covid19.pdf
8. https://www.equilar.com/blogs/345-ceo-hires-favor-insiders.html. In a 2018 Spencer Stuart CEO Transition analysis of S&P 500 firms, only 73% of the new CEOs were promoted from within. See: https://www.spencerstuart.com/research-and-insight/ceo-transitions-2018
9. LeBlanc (2016) and Spencer Stuart 2017. See: https://www.spencerstuart.com/research-and-insight/ceo-succession-planning-ceos-critical-role
10. Spencer Stuart, 2017. See: https://www.spencerstuart.com/research-and-insight/how-boards-can-overcome-the-most-common-succession-planning-obstacles
11. LeBlanc, R. 2016
12. Spencer Stuart, 2017. See: https://www.spencerstuart.com/research-and-insight/how-boards-can-overcome-the-most-common-succession-planning-obstacles
13. Spencer Stuart, 2019. See: https://www.spencerstuart.com/-/media/2019/march/ceo_transitions_2018_final.pdf?la=en&hash=5536FB72E90408EFA1A13D6F82006A0A090B3DCF. See Quigley and Hambrick noted in 2011

that 39% of retiring CEO's remained as board chair for an additional year and 26% stayed on for at least 3 years. See Quigley, T. J., & Hambrick, D. C. (2012). When the former CEO stays on as board chair: Effects on successor discretion, strategic change, and performance. *Strategic Management Journal*, 33(7), 834859.

14. Mandar Group is a fictitious company based on a composite of actual events at similar companies.
15. http://info.localytics.com/blog/4-ways-mobile-apps-are-transforming-the-banking-sector
16. https://www.edelman.com/research/trust-in-financial-services-2019
17. SEC Staff Legal Bulletin 14E, October 27, 2009. See: https://www.sec.gov/interps/legal/cfslb14e.htm
18. Holly Gregory - https://www.sidley.com/-/media/publications/mar16_govcounselor.pdf
19. At the same time, the board can request – during the subsequent interview process – that the leading potential successors take charge of these issues and present on them. Boards can see the candidates in action while making progress on the issues and opportunities that are important to the company's future.
20. Favaro, K., Karlsson, P. -O., & Neilson, G. L.. (2015, May 4). The $112 billion CEO Succession Problem. See: https://www.strategy-business.com/article/00327?gko=a813e
21. Spencer Stuart (2017). "How boards can overcome the most common succession planning obstacles." Available at: https://www.spencerstuart.com/research-and-insight/how-boards-can-overcome-the-most-common-succession-planning-obstacles
22. See https://www.linkedin.com/pulse/journey-unboss-how-were-learning-lead-differently-steven-baert/. See also Taylor, C. (2019), "Why the CEO of this multi-billion dollar firm wants to 'unboss' companies" Available at: https://www.cnbc.com/2019/10/29/why-novartis-ceo-wants-to-unboss-companies.html

6

CEO COMPENSATION

Once a board has identified potential successors, it can begin to design compensation plans that align their roles and training plans with incentives to stay with the organization. Thus, succession and compensation go hand in hand.

Publicly traded companies have long been mandated to have a compensation committee which, at a minimum, sets the pay and benefits for corporate executives, most notably the CEO. Most board compensation (or comp) committees spend the vast majority of their time focused on the firm's pay practices — including establishing competitive salary levels and crafting appropriate short- and long-term incentives that are intended to drive performance.

In setting a CEO's pay, the majority of firms use a compensation consultant and assemble a peer group including companies in similar business sectors and of comparable size and complexity.[1] This benchmarking allows the comp committee to target the total compensation package for the CEO with most choosing to target the median level (i.e., the 50th percentile). Proxy advisory firms like Glass Lewis and Institutional Shareholder Services (ISS) have created lists of their own peer groups. It's become a very big business. So much so that the SEC mandates disclosure and discussion of peer groups and targeted percentiles.[2] Interestingly, a recent study found that peer groups had a greater effect on pay increases than CEO performance did[3], and, in another study, researchers found that peer groups can be manipulated to include larger peer groups thus increasing pay.[4]

Much of what the comp committee does with regard to pay is currently in the spotlight. One of the most pivotal aspects are the disclosures in the Compensation Discussion and Analysis (CD&A) of a company's annual proxy statement. This section provides the narrative disclosure explaining all material elements of the company's executive compensation programs – the amount and type of compensation paid to its CEO, chief financial officer (CFO) and the three other most highly compensated executive officers. Also, according to the SEC's regulations, a company must disclose the criteria used in reaching executive compensation decisions and the relationship between the company's executive compensation practices and corporate performance.[5]

Typically, in a summary table format,[6] this disclosure includes information such as grants of stock options and stock appreciation rights, long-term incentive plan awards, pension plans, and employment contracts and related arrangements.[7]

The federal securities laws also require companies to put the disclosed pay of its executives to a vote by shareholders via what's called a "say-on-pay" vote.[8] The executive pay plans are subject to non-binding shareholder approval in the US and in many other countries globally, to a binding shareholder vote.[9] Regardless, each company must disclose in the CD&A whether, and how, its compensation policies and decisions have taken into account the results of the most recent say-on-pay vote.

Also, as part of the CD&A, a company typically discusses its compensation philosophy in the first part of this section of the proxy. According to one expert, this philosophy "can send a powerful message to outside constituents about the values of the company and how these values are reflected in the pay program".[10]

Perhaps, not surprisingly, the nature of CEO pay is changing in notable ways. For example, in September 2019, the Council of Institutional Investors (CII) altered its policy on executive compensation and urged others to similarly reduce the complexity of their pay plans and to, specifically, set longer periods for measuring performance for incentive awards. CIIs new policy urges companies to explore adopting simpler plans composed of salary and time-vesting restricted shares that vest over five years or more. Historically, a majority of time-vesting restricted stock awards have vested over three years. The policy also recommends that companies consider barring the CEO and CFO from selling stock awarded to them until after they depart, in order to ensure that management prioritizes the company's long-term success.[11] According to a study in the *Journal of Applied Corporate Finance*, 83% of S&P 500 companies offered long-term incentives (LTIs) paid as performance shares in 2018. That was up from 50% in 2009, and in fiscal year pay 2018, stock-based compensation comprised the majority of CEO pay at S&P 500 and S&P 400 companies for the first time.[12]

According to Pearl Meyer, a major compensation consulting firm, CEO pay is typically comprised of LTI elements but also short-term incentives (STIs) typically a target bonus for the CEO as a percentage of his or her salary (e.g., base pay). Total Direct Compensation (TDC) then has three components: base salary + STIs + LTIs.

With the prevalence of performance-based compensation, companies have evolved their selection of performance criteria. Long-term incentive plans use a wide variety of performance metrics at different weights, with total shareholder return or TSR, earnings and returns being the most popular performance-measuring categories. For short-term incentives, companies tend to use earnings, revenue and "other" company-specific criteria.[13]

While the core function of the comp committee in setting CEO pay remains relevant, some believe it is time to change the focus of the committee.[14] Major efforts in this area include broadening it to be responsible for the talent development for the all C-suite roles including crisis/emergency succession planning as well as diversity and inclusion initiatives. Another trend is to evaluate executives on their ability to meet various environmental, social and governance (ESG) metrics. Respondents to the 2020 NACD Public Company Governance Survey reported that investor discussions around ESG trended toward social issues, with an emphasis on human capital (65%) and diversity (74%). Yet, only 43% have reviewed charters to ensure that talent oversight responsibilities are effectively allocated across the board.[15] So, it would seem, talent management is everybody's and nobody's responsibility and, at the same time, incentivizing talent is an increasingly vital board role.

Board challenge #4: CEO compensation and the rising star

Apex Inc. is an S&P 500 cloud computing, software development and training company.[16] As one of only 32 (or 6.4%) of the female CEOs at S&P 500 companies, Kara Woolard has served as Apex's CEO for 5 years and is 57 years old.[17] At the October meeting, Apex's Human Capital and Compensation Committee ('comp') needs to decide on Kara's compensation package for the upcoming year.

Dwayne Norman is the Chair of Apex's comp committee. In a discussion with Dwayne, given her strong performance at the company, Kara explained she is looking for a package in line with the 75th percentile of the market. She mentioned her desire to remain with Apex but also noted that various headhunters have contacted her. Other factors Kara is likely aware of is the tight executive labor market and the comp committee's inability to identify solid internal candidates for succession.

In turn, Apex's board is happy with Kara's performance and wants to retain her. The company's total shareholder return (TSR) is positive – as is its return on assets and return on equity – which is on par with the broader indices for companies like Apex. However, relative TSR has lagged the company's peer group – despite few of those being seen as direct competitors – over the past 3- and 5-year periods. Her performance is aligned with the business strategy and she works well with the board, invites honest feedback and doesn't play favorites.

Furthermore, Kara has a high level of credibility with institutional investors and is well regarded by employees and the local community. As a high performing female CEO, Kara has numerous public speaking requests which she tries to accommodate but often must decline. She's become quite high profile having appeared frequently on market watch television news programs.

Apex's compensation philosophy has been to target the total direct compensation or TDC mostly at the market's 50% percentile. It will make adjustments for tenure, performance or other company-specific circumstances. For example, over the past few years, Apex has given bonus payouts that have ranged from 65% to 100% of its target based on performance. The board has also awarded Kara with notable increases over her 5-year tenure. Last year, her TDC was in the market's 55th percentile for last year, representing a 15% increase for Kara. Dwayne is aware that some on the committee are concerned about risk regarding say-on-pay if they were to award Kara in the 75% percentile that she is looking for.

Not only important is getting Kara's compensation right to Apex but also to proxy advisory firms that advise investors on how to vote their proxies. ISS, for example, looks at "relative degree of alignment", or RDA, which compares the percentile ranks of a company's CEO pay and company TSR performance relative to its peer group, as determined by ISS, over the prior 3-year period.[18] Generally, ISS believes a CEO pay-performance disconnect exists when CEO pay increases and TSR decreases in a given year. If the performance ranking against peers is much lower than the CEO pay ranking against peers, it can lead to heightened level of concern from ISS, disclosure of which is public. ISS creates a Governance Quality Score, which in part evaluates a firm's compensation practices. It includes this score in its proxy reports that provide the proxy advisor's say-on-pay vote recommendations. However, according to ISS, the Governance Quality Scores are disclosed alongside its proxy reports, but ISS claims they have no impact on its vote recommendations.[19]

Given the rise in shareholder proposals about the existence of the gender pay gap, ISS adopted a new case-by-case effort to address a company's voting policy for these proposals.[20] The new policy examines three aspects:

1. a company's policies and disclosures on diversity and inclusion, and whether its efforts lag behind its peers;
2. a company's compensation philosophy and use of fair and equitable practices; and
3. whether a company has been the subject of any recent controversies, litigation, or regulatory actions related to gender pay gap issues.

At Apex's last board meeting Dwayne shared with his committee the following chart of Kara's current compensation and comparative pay relative to Apex's peer group at the 25th, 50th, and 75th percentile. Market pay rates have increased due, in large part, to the tight labor market. Dwayne is aware that Kara's current pay is lower than the market's forecasted 50% percentile for next year and that it should be increased out of both a sense of equity but also the desire to keep her. But, he considered, what specifics should he discuss with the comp committee and ultimately present to the board?

Applying GVV

Place yourself in Dwayne's shoes and address the following:

(1) What is at stake for the parties involved?

To begin with, as is the case in giving voice to values, Dwayne is comfortable in his knowledge of what the right thing to do is – offer a fair and competitive compensation package to Kara Woolard, the CEO of Apex Inc. Dwayne, as the chair of the Human Capital and Compensation Committee has a stake in CEO compensation. Likewise, so do the shareholders, employees, regulators and consumers of Apex. How well the board handles a CEO's compensation has direct ramifications for the long- and short-term success of the company as well as the employee morale, especially among senior management. Simply put, what the comp committee does for Kara will have downstream consequences.

In the same way, it's also likely that other female CEOs and other female C-suite executives will also pay particular attention to the decision. Gender pay equity is a growing concern for multiple stakeholders and the perception might be that awarding Kara less is due to her being a woman. The general public is a key stakeholder here and there is much reputational risk for Apex. In all, this decision can leave Apex vulnerable to media attacks, shareholder activism and proxy advisor-heightened concern (e.g., ISS).

Dwayne's duties as a chair and as a director, have serious impacts for him and the stakeholders he serves. His duty of care requires him to address major business risks, including the departure of the CEO. With the fiduciary duty of loyalty, Dwayne faces the requirement to act in an independent manner with the good faith belief that his actions are in the best interest of the company. Given the board is in favor of retaining Kara and believes she has led the company well over the past 5 years, Dwayne's position in retaining her is in the best interest of Apex. Given the latitude in setting pay, directors have an obligation to exercise their discretion effectively. Relatedly, the comp committee of the board has a stake as it will be perceived as handling well, or not, its core duty.

Certainly, Kara also has a great deal at stake. As the first female CEO of Apex, and one of a small number in the entire S&P 500 index, many eyes are on her. Given she is only 57, however, it is reasonable to assume she has another CEO job in her future career. So, she has a rather easy exit plan in the event she doesn't get the pay she's negotiating. But also a salient point to consider – for both Kara and Dwayne – is the importance of Kara's firm-specific knowledge and the high cost of replacing a CEO.[21] Thus, there are pros and cons for Kara in staying with Apex. Empirical evidence in the academic literature, however, has found that an executive's skills are specific to the companies where they acquired them.[22] These considerations also impact the stakes involved.

Dwayne would be wise to find allies who may agree with him. The board has expressed a strong desire to keep Kara. The main decision is determining what pay package will achieve that while also considering what will help to motivate her. Of course, the latter is important for at least two reasons – it serves aspirational performance goals especially if tied to incentives and serves as a bridge to the next CEO in line (whom he also knows is not yet clear). Likewise, Dwayne might find allies among those on the comp committee given these are directors who share the same duties as he does in terms of mitigating future risk and doing what's best for the firm overall. Yet, he is aware that at least one member is a strong advocate for the use of peer groups and that a 75th percentile pay award will send up a red flag for ISS and some shareholders.

(2) *What are the reasons and rationalizations Dwayne needs to consider?*

Given the four most common rationalizations discussed throughout this book: (1) standard practice/status quo, (2) materiality, (3) locus of responsibility and (4) locus of loyalty, it seems the three that stand out for Dwayne most prominently are – standard practice, materiality, and locus of loyalty. It seems pretty clear that as comp committee chair, Dwayne and his committee are the key people responsible for this decision.

Let's start with standard practice. One of the most glaring issues here for Dwayne is the standard practice of using peer groups to determine executive pay. There is little question that some directors on the board, and one member of the comp committee, will likely argue that all firms use peer benchmarking for executive pay. Dwayne is aware he could bring up the point that Apex's peer group is not comprised of direct competitors given the company's broad technology space. This makes both the executive pay and the evaluation of Kara's performance difficult to determine with much precision. Standard practice is also likely to be an argument for not awarding Kara in the 75% as ISS is likely to issue a very public concern warning, and Apex's own compensation philosophy – of staying near the 50th percentile target – is certainly a standard practice at the firm but one that may not be effective in retaining Kara.

Dwayne needs to be prepared for why these standards of practice should be discussed further. For one, there is much research on the need to re-evaluate the use of peer groups. Likewise, shareholders elect directors for their judgment capabilities and not for their ability to follow formulas such as peer groups.[23] Also, peer group benchmarking creates structural bias for continually awarding higher and higher pay.[24] Lastly, Apex's own compensation philosophy allows for and acknowledges that the board of directors may need to tailor pay packages to company-specific circumstances (e.g., giving more than Apex's philosophy of awarding at the 50th percentile). Since its compensation philosophy says a lot about what it values, the standard practice argument takes on a larger meaning.

As for materiality, while some might argue that high executive pay doesn't hurt anyone, Dwayne needs to balance the desire to pay Kara appropriately with the potential damage to employee morale and motivation resulting from CEO compensation that is perceived to be too high. He could also bring up the high cost of replacing a CEO and the importance of awarding fair compensation as well. Likewise, Kara's pay, as a female executive, definitely matters to outside stakeholders who will undoubtedly flag the company for any perceived underpayment. The small number of female CEOs among the S&P 500 makes their pay highly scrutinized. And, there is little doubt that Kara's pay is important to the overall picture.

The rationalization of locus of loyalty is present in this case. To push back on potential questions about his loyalty, Dwayne can acknowledge that being loyal to his colleagues occurs when he stands up to them in voicing his values and beliefs about awarding Kara at the 75%, not the 50% level. The moral value of loyalty here is expressed in the form of being transparent with colleagues about his obligations and principles as a board member. Specifically, Dwayne needs to offer the counterpoint that Kara's good performance is indeed in line with most shareholder and other stakeholder expectations and it is best for those parties that Kara remain. Her pay should be fair and competitive, as such. In other words, Dwayne as a board member and chair of the comp committee may voice his values because he is loyal to the firm rather than in spite of it.

(3) Practicing and prescripting the response

There's the type of voicing our values that is about speaking up when we see conflicts of interest or dishonest behaviors in our firm. However, giving voice may also mean asking a well-constructed question, offering a new way of thinking, providing additional analyses or finding another way to accomplish a task that is more acceptable ethically. This type of voice describes what Dwayne is facing at Apex. In fact, there are a series of questions Dwayne feels he should ask related to Kara's pay as an initial way to exercise voice and his moral muscle. Such as:

1. Are the peer groups as objectively constructed as possible? If not, can we devise a new group and/or consult with ISS as to a more appropriate group, given Apex's unique tech space? (Note: this question is important for the comp committee member who favors peer groups.
2. How do we balance the cost of losing her, from a firm-specific knowledge standpoint, with the risk of the transferability of her skills to another firm?
3. Although her current pay approximated the market last year at the 55th percentile, is that possibly due to underpaying by gender? Or could it be perceived that way? Now that this year's market percentile amounts increased (see Figure 6.1), can we justify paying her at the same 55th percentile (i.e., increasing her pay by about $70k)? How does this compare to what we paid the previous (male) CEO? How does this put us at greater reputational risk or the risk of losing Kara?
4. When we think of future LTIs can we pay bonuses when certain objectives are met?
5. How can we best balance our desire to keep Kara and send a positive message to our employees with potentially inviting the ire of ISS with an award near the 75th percentile?
6. Is there a middle ground with STI and LTI somewhere between the 50th and the 75th percentile that seems fair and appropriate?
7. Because we want Kara to stay at Apex, should we focus more on LTI? How would this benefit (or not) our potential CEO succession planning of others in the C-suite?

Pay Component ($000s)	Kara Woolard's current pay	Market pay 25th %ile (next year)	Market pay 50th %ile (next year)	Market pay 75th %ile (next year)
Base Salary	$850	$800	$900	$1,000
STI: target bonus (% of salary)	125%	100%	$125%	$150%
Total Cash Comp	$1,913	$1,600	$2,025	$2,500
LTI: 3 yr target	$6,500	$4,500	$6,000	$8,000
TDC	$8,413	$6,100	$8,025	$10,500

Figure 6.1 Next year's CEO market pay rates.

For Dwayne, or perhaps anyone else in this delicate situation, voice may be soft or loud and is by no means always an overt protest. Since he knows at least one director on the compensation committee is a fan of peer groups, Dwayne decides to focus on generating suggestions and addressing key concerns or opinions.[25] In this regard, he decides to use these questions, as a sequential road map of sorts, so as to move the conversation toward making a set of pay component suggestions using the table he previously circulated (i.e., Figure 6.1).

He decides to start with the 1st question above in order to get the comp committee to engage in a conversation about peer group efficacy. He reasons – if he can get the comp committee to minimize the use of the peer group – he can gain greater latitude in what is ultimately offered to Kara. He decides to use some of the information on peer groups presented earlier (in this board challenge) to discuss some of the problems with their use. Also, there is the disclosure to the SEC describing Apex's use of peer groups he must consider. One of his main points here is that while metrics from peer groups are helpful, they are not as objective as they might appear. They are simply one data point among many. Apex's comp committee may be best served by using its own independent judgment based on the subjective factors about Kara herself given that the compensation at the top is a central component of the broader corporate culture at Apex. He knows the board must be mindful of the impact this process and outcome could have on employee morale, especially among women top executives, and decides to work that into the conversation.[26]

Relatedly, he is aware that, ultimately, the board will need to consider the shareholder vote of the pay plan as well as the reputational issues in the media given Kara is only one of a small number of female CEOs. He expects he will need to give his opinion of what Kara's exact pay components should look like. Here, he needs to flesh out what elements of STI and LTI are appropriate and offer a specific suggestion for the amount of Kara's TDC. He reasons that somewhere in the middle of the 50th and 75th percentile is a starting point of the conversation.

(4) Board Exercise

In order to extend the lessons learned with this board challenge, consider having each board member prepare an actual script for Dwayne to use with the comp committee. Then, have your fellow board members evaluate each other's script draft anonymously. Think about:

- What are its strengths and weaknesses?
- What are the key messages and key arguments?
- How effective do you think it will be?
- How would you improve Dwayne's approach? Can you take elements of several scripts?

Conclusion

There is a great deal of board-level discretion in executive pay, but at the same time, it is highly scrutinized in the media and among the other players, like proxy advisory firms and shareholders, in the broader market. Some companies, like Tesla, have been sued repeatedly over executive compensation.[27] Part of a director's job, therefore, is to shed some light on issues and policies that are subject to interpretation, and to provide a way to frame the challenge at hand, such as the one Dwayne finds himself in with Kara Woolard's compensation. Practicing your overall approach and prescripting, as this board challenge asks us to do, is a key way to develop the necessary moral muscle board members need when determining executive pay.

However, as the scrutiny on executive compensation continues to intensify, there is a greater expectation for fairness and shared sacrifice as a result of the COVID-19 pandemic and its impact on employees, shareholders, and other stakeholders. Proxy advisors ISS and Glass Lewis weighed in and asked companies to contemporaneously disclose changes to employment, compensation and benefits during COVID-19.

While leaders at companies across the globe implemented strategies to guide their organizations through the pandemic, the spotlight was and continues to be on CEOs and how they respond. While there are many, boards could follow the example of Signet Jeweler's (NYSE: SIG) very comprehensive response regarding executive pay during COVID-19. CEO Virginia Drosos took a temporary 50% reduction in base salary.[28] Additional actions included (1) reduction of salary with partial exchange for stock; (2) splitting of annual bonus into two halves, with the first half based on liquidity; (3) a reweighting of equity grants towards more time-based awards; (4) delay of the performance share grant until a time when it might be easier to set; and (5) freezing of deferred compensation matching.

The takeaway is that some corporate leaders are willing to take significant steps to help mitigate and ease the financial burden faced by their organizations. As developments from this and other recent crises continue to play out, the question then is when and how to adjust executive pay when employees continue to be layed-off.

Notes

1. Elson, C. M., & Ferrere, C. K. (2016). Peer groups: understanding CEO compensation and a proposal for a new approach. *The Handbook of Board Governance: A Comprehensive Guide for Public, Private and Not-for-Profit Board Members*, 461-473.
2. Elson & Ferrere (2016).
3. Bizjak, J., Lemmon, M., & Nguyen, T. (2011). Are all CEOs above average? An empirical analysis of compensation peer groups and pay design. *Journal of Financial Economics*, 100(3), 538555.
4. Bizjak, J., Lemmon, M., & Nguyen, T. (2011)
5. See SEC investor information available at: https://www.sec.gov/fast-answers/answers-execomphtm.html

   Note: Another issue in the spotlight a provision addressing the demand for more accountability within the context of executive compensation is the Rule 10D-1 "clawback" under the Dodd-Frank Act. The proposal, made in 2015 but not yet finalized, would require: (1) current and former executives return incentive-based pay awarded within three years prior to an accounting restatement and (2) that companies disclose their recovery procedures in the annual report.

6. Andrews Kurth's 2018 "CEO Pay Ratio Disclosure: What We've Seen in Filings So Far". Note: many of the proxy statements include the pay ratio disclosure right after the summary compensation table and related tables and before the director compensation section. This placement is logical because the disclosure is kept out of the CD&A and is, therefore, not subject to the Compensation Committee certification.
7. U.S. Securities & Exchange Commission. Executive Compensation Investor Information. See: https://www.sec.gov/fast-answers/answers-execomphtm.html
8. U.S. Securities & Exchange Commission. See: https://www.sec.gov/fast-answers/answers-execomphtm.html. Numerous cities and states have considered or are considering special taxes, surtaxes or fees on companies with "excessive" CEO pay ratios (CA, CT, MA, MN, NY, RI) see Choate deck
9. Hall, S., McCord, N., & Hall, S. (2016). The Effective Compensation Committee. *The Handbook of Board Governance: A Comprehensive Guide for Public, Private and Not-for-Profit Board Members*, 474500.
10. Hall, McCord & Hall (2016).
11. CFO.com "Performance-based pay comes under fire". September 25, 2019. See: https://www.cfo.com/compensation/2019/09/performance-based-pay-comes-under-fire/
12. Harvard Law School Forum on Corporate Governance. See: https://corpgov.law.harvard.edu/2019/04/16/2019-u-s-executive-compensation-trends/
13. Harvard Law School Forum on Corporate Governance. See: https://corpgov.law.harvard.edu/2019/04/16/2019-u-s-executive-compensation-trends/
14. Alan J. Kaplan, Bank Director.com "Why the compensation committee need a rebrand." November 6, 2019. See: https://www.bankdirector.com/committees/compensation/why-the-compensation-committee-needs-a-rebrand/
15. See NACD Risk Oversight Advisory Council: Current and Emerging Practices in Cyber-Risk Oversight (June 2019). Available at: https://www.nacdonline.org/insights/content.cfm?ItemNumber=66907

16. Apex Inc. is a fictitious company based on a composite of actual events at similar companies.
17. Catalyst Research 2020. List: Women CEOs of the S&P 500. Available at https://www.catalyst.org/research/women-ceos-of-the-sp-500/ Figures are as of December 2019
18. Davis-Polk (2018), A say on pay update. See: https://www.davispolk.com/files/2018-11-29-a_say-on-pay_update_plus_strategies.pdf
19. Davis-Polk (2018)
20. Wanless, L., 2017. ISS Policy changes for 2018 put more scrutiny on CEO pay-for-performance and director pay. See: https://radford.aon.com/insights/articles/2017/iss-policy-changes-for-2018-put-more-scrutiny-on-ceo-pay-for-performance-and-director-pay
21. According to Soencer Stuart, the economic cost of appointing the wrong CEO at global companies is estimated at more than $100 billion. See: https://www.spencerstuart.com/research-and-insight/ceo-selection—the-costs-of-getting-it-wrong#footnote1
22. Elson, C. M., & Ferrere, C. K. (2016). Peer groups: understanding CEO compensation and a proposal for a new approach. *The Handbook of Board Governance: A Comprehensive Guide for Public, Private and Not-for-Profit Board Members*, 461473.
23. Elson & Ferrere (2016).
24. Ibid.
25. Morrison, E. W. 2011. Employee voice behavior: Integration and directions for future research. *Academy of Management Annals*, 5: 373412.
26. Gender affects diversity both from the board up and the board down. Greater gender equality at the top level of organizations contributes to equality at lower managerial levels (Matsa, D. A., & Miller, A. R. (2011). Chipping away at the glass ceiling: gender spillovers in corporate leadership. *American Economic Review*, 101, 635–639). Also, gender diversity on boards is positively associated with the appointment and success of women CEOs (Cook, A., & Glass, C. (2015). Diversity begets diversity. The effects of board composition on the appointment and success of women CEOs. *Social Science Research*, 53, 137–147). In addition, it has been found that the gender gap in executive compensation is smaller when there are more women on boards and on compensation committees (Shin, T. (2012). The gender gap in executive compensation: The role of female directors and

chief executive officers. *Annals of the American Academy of Political and Social Science*, 639, 258–278).

27. Szymkowski, S. 2020. Elon Musk, Tesla board sued over alleged excessive compensation. CNET. See: https://www.cnet.com/roadshow/news/elon-musk-tesla-board-sued-compensation-salary-pay-package/
28. See SEC DEF 14A disclosure. Available at: https://www.sec.gov/Archives/edgar/data/832988/000083298820000070/fy20definitiveproxydocument.htmA

7

DIGITAL INNOVATION AND THE BOARDROOM

Spencer Stuart – a global executive search and board advisory firm – noted in a recent survey that corporate boards are grappling with how to ensure that the risks and opportunities emerging from a diverse set of digital forces — ranging from *artificial intelligence* and robotics to cybersecurity, data science and e-commerce — are fully understood by directors and factored into a business's strategy.[1] Further, these forces are becoming more and more integrated. According to the World Economic Forum (WEF), developments in previously disjointed fields such as artificial intelligence and machine learning, robotics, nanotechnology, 3D genetics and biotechnology are all building on and amplifying one another.

Due to these rapid technological advances, business strategies are changing to accommodate the meaningful reductions in transaction and engagement costs. Sometimes, this results in products, services, and business models needing to be reinvented in real time. According to the WEF, cloud technology and big data are two of the top industry drivers of change and disruptions to business models identified by the senior executives in its Future of Jobs survey, ranked according to the share of respondents who expected each trend to be among the top trends impacting their industry.

Yet, while these innovations pose a real threat to business as we know it today, 61% of the directors who responded to the 2020 NACD survey report they would be willing to compromise on cybersecurity to achieve business objectives, while only 28% prioritize cybersecurity above all else. Additionally, cybersecurity experience was cited in only 2% of newly appointed directors while human capital management was present in just 3% of newly appointed directors,[2] and the pace at which digital innovation and diffusion is taking place is far faster than governments and regulators can keep up with.[3]

Therefore, as governance professionals, we might be in the midst of a perfect storm where a number of issues need the board's attention at the same time. IT governance includes oversight of both cybersecurity but also how technology can drive value for the firm.[4] IT governance, if done properly, helps the board fulfill its duty of care, outlined above. In fact, many boards are focused on defining the link between ESG and risk, sort of a meeting point for IT governance.

Given the board's responsibility with regard to overall enterprise risk management, and the growing issue of cyber risk specifically, we will focus in this chapter on likely types of cyber incidents and how both the firm's board of directors and its consumers see them. In addition, we will practice how to use the GVV framework in navigating a likely scenario facing a board with regard to customer data usage.

A cyber incident is a violation of some aspect of the firm's security policy (e.g., unauthorized access to personal information, improper use, storage or processing of data). *Security* is about protecting *personal information* (PI), while *privacy* is broader and encompasses the permission and use of personal information. Privacy is difficult to achieve without security. PI means information that identifies, relates to, describes, is capable of being associated with, or could reasonably be linked, directly or indirectly, with a particular consumer or household. For example, these include identifiers such as a real name, alias, postal address, unique personal identifier, online identifier, Internet Protocol address, email address, account name, Social Security number, driver's license number, passport number or other similar identifiers.[5]

However, organizations can successfully secure the personal information in their custody and still make bad decisions about how the personal information they have collected is subsequently used.[6] Given the vast amount of personal information generated by millions of consumer transactions each day, there can be serious privacy problems resulting from the storage, analysis, use, or sharing of this information. The extensive use of increasingly more data—often personal, often sensitive—and the growing reliance on algorithms to analyze them in order to shape choices and to make decisions (i.e., artificial intelligence) are at the root of the harmful effects of collecting PI. What's more, some experts believe there has been a gradual reduction of human involvement in these automatic processes and that they, too, pose pressing concerns about fairness, rights and responsibilities.

However, there are also many benefits to collecting and using such information. For example, noted privacy researchers Kathleen Greenaway and Yolande Chan showed that an organization's information privacy behaviors can help a firm achieve legitimacy and can provide a strategic advantage to an organization.[7] Also, the vast amounts of information that can be mined may offer firms a new product line or service and, as a result, a new revenue stream. However, such opportunities need to be considered alongside the ethical challenges that may result and boards will need to become accustomed to dealing with both of these aspects.

Information reuse and unauthorized access

Let's zero-in on a few key issues for boards arising from the way organizations process PI: information reuse and unauthorized access to personal information. Typically, *information reuse* involves organizations making legal decisions about new uses for the PI they collect, while *unauthorized access* represents activities that violate either laws or corporate policies. Both activities – information reuse and unauthorized access – can potentially threaten a consumer's ability to maintain limited access to his or her personal information. Both can also cause harm to individuals and subsequently threaten the organization's legitimacy in its interactions with consumers, shareholders, and regulators.[8]

Additionally, what starts out as authorized access can create privacy and security issues. PWC reports that 63% of all cyber attacks could be traced either directly or indirectly to third parties, like application developers,[9] and these third parties often maintain less stringent security protocols, raise fewer suspicions and allow for easier identity masking — providing ideal points of entry for attackers looking to leverage unauthorized access.

While companies see the importance in collecting and analyzing the data of consumers, they also see the risks. Calls for better privacy protection face a daunting set of fragmented laws and regulations, which are often country specific, making it challenging for companies to comply.[10]

In the United States, as of this writing, there is no federal level law covering consumer privacy rights. The U.S. Federal Trade Commission (FTC), which has responsibility for enforcing fair trade practices in privacy and data use, recommends that businesses offer consumers greater disclosure and simple opt-out tools, but there is yet no legislation enacted by Congress that enforces these practices. This lack of collaboration between the FTC and Congress creates a gap between what PI is expected to be protected and what businesses are actually doing in regard to collecting data. COVID-19, and containment efforts that rely on personal data, are also shining a spotlight on this longstanding problem.

In 2012, the White House proposed the Consumer Privacy Bill of Rights and in 2015 proposed the Consumer Privacy Act, however Congress enacted neither into law. Without success on the Federal level, states began to consider the issue on their own. On June 28, 2018 the California State Legislature passed a law known as the California Consumer Privacy Act (CCPA), which went into effect January 1, 2020 and aims to provide Californian citizens and residents with more information about how companies collect their personal data, outlining several rights to PI. Fines are enforced by the California Attorney General and can reach up to $7,500 per violation (in the case of intentional violations).[11] Non-intentional violations remain subject to a $2,500 maximum fine. Several other states in the US are considering similar laws, and India, China, Russia, Canada and Brazil all adopted privacy laws in 2018.[12]

Unlike the uncertainty of PI collection in the US, the European Union has recently placed strict regulations on businesses in regard to using big data. This law, called the General Data Protection Regulation (GDPR), prevents companies from collecting and processing any data that can be connected to an identifiable person without prior consent. In addition, individuals have the ability to block companies from collecting their data and using it for profiling purposes.[13] Implemented in May of 2018, the GDPR has also imposed conditions on how the information is stored and for how long.

In fact, one of the key differences of the GDPR and the CCPA is the data collection consent aspect. GDPR specifically requires consumers to opt-in, or to consent to data collection *before* the site collects the data. The CCPA offers consumers only the right to opt-out, where companies make available information about how they collect, use, and share personal information and allow individuals to opt out if they desire. While there are pros and cons to each approach, experts generally agree that opt-in privacy rules create a greater sense of control over PI.[14]

In a recent 2-year study by the Pew Research Center, a non-partisan organization that informs the public about the issues, attitudes, and trends shaping the world, 91% of adults agree or strongly agree that consumers have lost control of how personal information is collected and used by companies.[15] This control over PI remains a hot button issue for consumers and one that all boards need to pay attention to as it is likely to remain an issue or become more likely to grow in importance.

Board challenge #5: cybersecurity or digital innovation?

Grupo, a public company, is a very successful social media platform specializing in connecting groups of friends with multiple other friends, creating billions of online community groups, networks and social exchanges.[16] Not only can users easily create their own personal profiles, list friends and search others' friends, the platform can easily accept applications ("apps") which allow third party developers to create special features that work within the platform such as photo sharing, video streaming and personal event timelines.

The data Grupo collects is voluminous and only continuing to grow. It starts when a user creates an account by revealing their name, gender, date of birth, email or phone number and other personal information. Once they start using Grupo, the company gathers data about what customers click on, "like", or share. Each user's data profile is constantly updated every time they add information (e.g., schools attended, vacations planned, books read, children born, etc.). Importantly, Grupo keeps a "user log" for each user that stores all of their activity from the moment they created the account. This data includes photos of people who were "tagged" by others, adding or deleting friends, connections made over the years and searches for other people and pages.

Since joining Grupo is free, the company makes money in two interrelated ways: selling advertising space and monetizing the vast amounts of data it collects on users. Advertisers on social media want the space with the most viewers in order to increase their engagement with those specifically targeted customers. This engagement is measured using metrics such as "likes", "shares" and "reposts" of a user's voluntarily uploaded information. The more likes and shares a post receives, the more valuable the space is for advertisers and the more money Grupo makes.

Grupo's business model is optimized for maximum returns: it has no cost for content because consumers generate the content, no marketing costs because users speak with each other about their experiences or life events and minimal costs to sell the advertising space because its ad service is do-it-yourself. More specifically, Grupo allows other businesses, such as third-party app developers, to create and manage their own ads, find tools to help them target specific audiences, track results and make changes all without ever interacting with a person at Grupo. Grupo offers a special analytics tool to these app developers, which allows them to see statistics about users' activities, and to target those users with advertisements. Grupo has been very focused on increasing the company's user base and adding advertisers and is currently the dominant social networking platform.

With regard to user's especially sensitive PI data, such as health, financial or sexual information, Grupo sorts through the vast amounts of data to get advertisers the specific audience they are looking to reach. Attempts are made to "depersonalize" the information to keep it private and secure. Grupo's CEO, Alex Magnet, has said several times, the company does not share users' personal data with advertisers. In fact, a few weeks ago Grupo changed its privacy policy to include an online privacy tool that guided users through the configuration of their own personal privacy settings and included Grupo's recommendations.

Recently, a high-profile newspaper reporter from the *Wall Street Journal* has been poking around Grupo's privacy policy and the access to data. Steve Strayed reported that despite Grupo's claims that the company does not share users' PI with advertisers, it allowed them access to personal information when a user clicked on an ad on their event timeline. Further, the article claimed that developers had the ability to display this personal user information to others on their own site, regardless of those users' privacy settings (e.g., even when a user's privacy settings were not set to share with everyone and even when the user had deleted their account altogether). In short, the article accuses Grupo of deceiving users and improperly managing their personal data. The article states, authorities believe the company failed to protect personal information by allowing a third-party app to access users' data.

These allegations came as a shock to Samantha Yang, the chair of the audit committee of the board of directors at Grupo. Samantha liked to think of herself as an engaged director and one who knows her stuff, but this allegation made her think about whether she was too complacent, or worse, in violation of her fiduciary duty of care. However, even though it's a rarity on boards, Samantha felt strongly that she was a tech savvy person. Recently, she had been considering contacting her colleagues on the nominating committee to begin a dialogue about searching for directors with cybersecurity knowledge and experience.

Immediately after the *Journal* article came out, the board of directors at Grupo created a special committee to investigate the situation. The committee immediately met with the CEO and other senior executives as well. As a result, the scope of the problem, albeit complex, began to emerge.

CEO Alex Magnet discussed how his management team was largely focused on increasing the company's user base and adding advertisers – especially in the face of a growing set of new and formidable competitors – and may have become less diligent over time about enforcing its data-use rules. But when further pressed by Samantha, Alex admitted that the new privacy tool guides users through the configuration so that the system recommends — via a default preselect — the setting to share the content users post to Grupo, such as status messages and wall posts, with everyone on the Internet, versus being limited to people identified as in their "networks" or as "friends".

Furthermore, under its current privacy policy, Grupo treats that information — along with name, profile picture, current city, gender, networks, and the pages that a user is a "fan" of — as "publicly available information" or "PAI", not personal information, or PI, as defined above. People become fans of many issues, some of them controversial, and may not want others outside their network of friends to know. For example, a user might become a fan of a page that supports or condemns the legalization of marijuana, and they want their personal friends see this on their profile, but may want to hide it from their co-workers, relatives or the public at large.

Users used to be allowed to restrict access to much of that information, however Grupo's major privacy settings are now set to share with everyone by default, unless the user changes it. Likewise, apps made by developers can obtain all information designated as PAI, for example, whenever a friend adds an app to their profile. Alex explained Grupo made this change because it noticed that very few users actually selected the privacy option that limited information to just networks or friends.

Samantha was stunned but wanted to make absolutely sure she understood exactly what had been going on. In the back of her mind, she was intent on asking the right questions as part of her board duties.

She asked Alex:

> *"Did Grupo share user information like photos and videos, with outside app developers - even if the user deactivated or deleted their account and despite promising users it would never share their information in this manner?" "Yes" was the answer.*

Samantha followed up:

> *"So, did we assume that the privacy tool prompts constituted user consent?" "Yes" again.*

At this moment, it became clear to Samantha that the company, at best, had repeatedly been too slow to react to privacy and security issues that consumers care about. And, at worst, the company was unclear with its consumers and may be in violation the FTC guidelines for proper disclosure of data usage, not to mention the CCPA and GDPR laws in terms of user consent. She knew such a violation could result in large fines or a lawsuit from the Federal Trade Commission, in the US, as well as a class-action lawsuit from shareholders.

The board went on to discuss other challenges to data collection and use. The conversation centered around the fact that companies today rely on a broad range of third-party vendors to support core business functions, which typically entails granting these third-party entities access to a company's data and its internal systems. This digital interconnectivity between vendor and customer creates an inherent risk.

It was at this point that Samantha felt she knew what the right thing to do is and now she needed to think through the options for addressing it.

Applying GVV

Using the GVV framework, place yourself in Samantha's shoes and address the following:

- What's at *stake* for the key parties, including those who disagree with Samantha Yang? How can she find *allies* among those who may agree with her?
- What are the main arguments Samantha and the board, is trying to counter? That is, what are the reasons and rationalizations she needs to address?
- What is her most powerful and persuasive response to the reasons and rationalizations needing to be addressed? To whom should the argument be made? When and in what context?

(1) What is at stake for the parties involved?

To begin with, as is the case in giving voice to values, Samantha Yang is comfortable in her knowledge of what the right thing to do is – Grupo must obtain clear consent for the use of PI and disclose the error to its users.

Samantha, as the chair of the audit committee, has a stake in risk oversight, although the direct oversight remains unclear as Grupo has not set up a stand-alone risk committee. Like all committees, the work undertaken is only as good as the information it gets from management. On this aspect, the senior management team – specifically the CEO and the Chief Risk Officer (CRO) – have obvious and significant duties regarding what happens following the *Wall Street Journal* article. Still, whether there is a specific committee or not, the governance of enterprise information and technology is a board-wide responsibility.[17]

Likewise, shareholders, employees, regulators and the consumers of Grupo have stakes in both how this issue is handled at this moment and in the future. How well or poorly the board handles reputational risk management has direct ramifications for the long- and short-term success of the company, especially because of the social media space Grupo occupies. Therefore, what Grupo does now is of great interest to the entire industry, lest they be tarred with the same brush and people lose faith. The general public, specifically Grupo's future user base, is a key stakeholder here and there is much reputational risk for the social media giant – as well as for its industry competitors. In all, this decision can leave Grupo vulnerable to media attacks, shareholder activism, increased regulation, potential fines and unwanted proxy advisor attention. Upcoming changes in regulations in the US and in Europe are putting pressure on boards to manage risk oversight effectively.

Samantha's duties as the audit chair and as a board member directly impact her decision to voice her values on behalf of the company she serves. Simply put, her duty of care requires Samantha to address major business risks, including the access to and use of PI. Samantha faces the requirement to act in good faith and in the best interest of the company. Consumers have entrusted Grupo with their personal information and if it mishandles it, the company's interest in retaining its leadership position in the industry would likely be compromised.

(2) *What are the reasons and rationalizations Samantha Yang needs to consider?*

While there are others, we've focused on four categories when it comes to rationalizations discussed throughout this book: (1) standard practice/ status quo, (2) materiality, (3) locus of responsibility, and (4) locus of loyalty, it seems all four apply to this board challenge.

Let's start with standard practice. One of the most glaring issues here for Samantha is the standard practice given the confusing array of laws and jurisdictions. She also knew the arguments for there being no clear law in the US due to the lack of collaboration between the FTC and Congress. Regardless of whether Grupo is headquartered in California, or in Europe, Samantha is well aware that some of the data collected were from citizens living in those areas – and clear consent was not given via the default preselect on Grupo's new privacy tool. She knows, too, that she will need to pay attention to emerging best practices as the nature of PI and user consent is mercurial. Also, a growing trend in all areas of business is the existence of a big gap between what PI citizens expect to be protected and what businesses are actually doing in regard to collecting data. So, there is a glaring need to be prepared for why these standards of practice exist and if they are the best practices available. Samantha should integrate any alternative best practices into her script.

As for materiality, some on the board might argue that the default, which sets the information to PAI, is due to the fact that the company found its users don't choose to select other options. Thus, they may reason, the default doesn't hurt anyone. Yet, this position will undoubtedly need to be balanced with the desire to reap high advertising revenue from the PAI with the potential to compromise or even damage a user's trust or reputation as a result. Also relevant are the high cost of litigation, regulatory fines and reputational risk from Grupo's perspective.

A third customary rationalization involves one's locus of responsibility – our sense of who we think should act in a given situation or who is requiring us to act. It seems clear in this situation that at a minimum shareholders, regulators and customers would require the board to act. Still, sometimes we hear people claim they are not the appropriate person to handle the situation, or do not possess the requisite authority to remedy the issue. Some might even find it in their best interest to deny their authority over the issue. This rationalization seems to hit at the heart of Samantha Yang's role on the Grupo board. Although she is the chair of the audit committee it is plausible that, given its numerous other duties, the committee does not have the time or the skills to oversee risk in addition. This is both a rationalization and an oversight by the board in its structuring of various committees. Samantha should expect that other directors may also use this rationalization in order to reduce their personal accountability, or further argue that their actions result from the CEO who has the control over the decision to make user consent unclear. She may hear other directors claiming they are not the appropriate person to handle the situation, or do not possess the requisite authority to remedy the issue or are simply following directions. Yet, she is aware the duty of loyalty obligates directors to act independently, especially of the CEO and his interests. Relatedly, acting in good faith requires that directors take action as opposed to turning a blind eye in the interest of their duty of care. This rationalization may manifest itself in someone claiming the government regulators bear the responsibility given the patchwork of laws making oversight unclear.

The rationalization of locus of loyalty is present in this case as well. Samantha and her fellow directors must balance the tension between short- and long-term goals of the company – as some shareholders may see benefits to leveraging user data while others do not. But as she can point out, these are only perceived to be divided loyalties. Samantha needs to offer the counterpoint that Grupo's good performance is indeed in line with shareholder and other stakeholder expectations about PI and it is best for those parties that transparency of user PI is a priority now and in the long term. Likewise, doing so may avoid hits to revenue over the long term due to customers defecting for platforms which are more concerned about users' privacy. In terms of loyalty, we acknowledge the very real possibility that loyalty can be a form of action which exists alongside using one's voice. In other words, as with other directors, Samantha's role as a board member may require voicing her values because she is loyal to the firm rather than in spite of it.

(3) Practicing and prescripting the response

Samantha Yang decided she needed find her allies on the board, despite their lack of cybersecurity expertise. In fact, her duty of care requires that she do so. Also, she reasoned, they might still become allies if she could somehow prepare the roots, as it were, for a more fruitful conversation to grow eventually. Her first thought was to contact her fellow audit committee members. She felt the CRO and the CEO had already made the decision to use PI and to set the privacy default settings to benefit the company not the user, they were likely to rationalize their choice, and they appeared to be holding back key information from the board already. However, just because the CEO and CRO appear to have already made a decision does not mean that she cannot begin to try to re-frame, influence, even nudge them especially after garnering allies on the committee. She also decided to contact her friend and legal advisor who had counseled her when she first joined the Grupo board. The two of them spent hours crafting a persuasive argument, a "script" if you will, for her approach to the board. Both felt the right context was to first call a meeting of the audit committee and then to present her script to the entire board.

One aspect on her mind, especially in her effort to gain allies on the audit committee, was how to frame the concern so that it didn't feel like an attack on Alex, the CEO, but more of a risk the whole board wants to avoid. She felt that one way to do this was to illustrate the need for both management and the board to reassess their cybersecurity acumen in light of the *Wall Street Journal's* very public and negative assessment of that acumen. Samantha knew that Grupo is not alone in needing this reassessment but thought focusing on the article was a more neutral way of bringing up the issue facing Grupo. She knows recent analysis of the issue bears this out. According to the 2020 NACD report, cybersecurity experience was cited in only 2% of newly appointed directors while human capital management was present in just 3% of newly appointed directors.[18] However, she stressed that while this could be perceived as standard practice at many firms, Grupo's high-profile position in the tech industry makes these topics and concerns central to its management and board roles.

Once in front of the board, and having consulted with the audit committee, Samantha focused on empathizing with the consumer. She started by using an attention grabber – that consumers remain skeptical about how companies are using data. In an April 2018 Harris Poll survey of more than 10,000 global consumers, 78% said that a company's ability to protect their data was extremely important, and 75% said they would not buy a product, no matter how good, from a company if they didn't trust the company to protect their data.[19]

Additionally, she noted, companies face increasing tensions between the revenue opportunities from utilizing data and the pressures to protect personal privacy. There has been considerable debate about this issue in recent years. New legal requirements have emerged, making privacy protection an important compliance imperative. At the same time, the issue goes beyond compliance to include the less explicit, but still significant, considerations associated with safeguarding a company's reputation and trustworthiness in the eyes of customers, employees and the public.

She reiterated that CCPA gives consumers the right to be informed regarding what information has been collected about them, rights to data access and portability, and the right to have their personal information deleted. The law also expands the definition of personal information to include location and browsing history.[20] Samantha reiterated her concern about honoring a user's privacy settings and not sharing data without a user's explicit permission.

Samantha summed up Grupo's challenge – customers have high expectations in this area. The onus is on every company to provide transparency, process data fairly, and be accountable. Grupo needs to clearly explain how and why the default settings were set up whether that was the right way to obtain consent. Well-formulated consent policies help minimize risk – and in the case of personal information it needs to be explicit and informed consent.[21] Ideally, it should not be buried in a default setting. We also need to immediately reverse the default settings to allow users to determine what information is part of PAI versus the information they wish to allow only their approved friends to see.

Then she raised a new point about the need to actively seek out the information the board needs in order to provide monitoring. Grupo should be contacting the management team on the implications of its approach to cyber policies, processes and even incentives to assess our potential blind spots, she explained, and there is an immediate need to evaluate the expertise and talent necessary to execute the Grupo's cybersecurity strategy.[22] This includes at the board level as well. This discussion, she explained, was already conducted within the audit committee, but is also important for the board as a whole.

Lastly, Samantha expressed her concerns about the extent to which the board should focus more on this issue going forward. Having an IT-risk response process with clear roles and responsibilities and regular reporting in place helps to demonstrate its duty of care. But she wanted to make sure the board had made a good faith effort to implement an oversight system and then monitor it. She also believed that by carefully reviewing the results of the special committee's reports, while remaining personally involved in the firm remedies, they could protect themselves as well as Grupo's reputation.

(4) ***Board Exercise***

In order to extend the lessons learned with this board challenge, consider these questions at your next board meeting:

- How would you evaluate Samantha's script? What are its strengths and weaknesses?
- What are the key messages she is trying to send? What are the key arguments she is trying to address?
- How effective do you think she will be?
- Does Samantha need to "rescript" and redesign her action plan? Or, does your board context necessitate doing so?

To what extent do you agree or disagree with the following statements?

Statement					
My board's understanding of cyber risks today has significantly improved, to two years ago.	6%	12%	53%	28%	
Collectively, my board's understanding of cyber risks is strong enough to provide effective oversight.	13%	28%	48%	10%	
My own understanding of cyber risks is strong enough to provide effective oversight.	15%	33%	42%	10%	
I am confident that our company is properly secured against a cyberattack.	11%	38%	44%	6%	

Strongly disagree
Disagree
Neither agree nor disagree
Agree
Strongly agree

Figure 7.1 Board preparedness for cyber risk.

Conclusion

This case is based on high-profile social media firms experiencing similar crises regarding user PI data over the past several years. As a result, many experts have weighed in on this issue and most agree companies like Grupo must take the time to establish a clear protocol for handling customer data and customer consent. The policies on data usage need to be viewed and reviewed often and to the extent the management team itself is deficient in terms of the necessary skills, the board must engage with members of the executive team around this issue. The board may even need greater visibility into critical areas of their companies' workforce in order to address these areas of weakness. According to a recent NACD survey, these deficiencies are commonplace (see Figure 7.1).[23]

In some instances, US firms have entered into agreements with regulators to create an independent privacy committee on which board directors, employees and the CEO are disqualified from serving. These committees are typically required to be briefed about all material privacy risks and have approval-and-removal authority over the compliance officer, or independent assessor, who does not answer to the company.

One aspect Samantha may have overlooked is the need for a continuous and careful review of Grupo's reasons for the retention of PI and the creation a records' retention schedule, taking great care to document the business justifications for a given retention period. Likewise, firms need to ensure personal information is being deleted regularly according to the retention schedule. Firms and their boards should review the business processes involving PI and determine systematically when deletion is required by law. Data usage and privacy concerns will continue to be an issue for boards as evidenced by the near daily coverage of such issues in all major news outlets.

Notes

1. Spencer Stuart, 2019. The digital dilemma: Optimizing board composition in the digital era. See: https://www.spencerstuart.com/-/media/2019/february/digitalexpertboard-013019.pdf
2. NACD Risk Oversight Advisory Council: Current and Emerging Practices in Cyber-Risk Oversight (June 2019). See: https://www.nacdonline.org/insights
3. Economist Joseph Schumpeter introduced the idea of a three-part trilogy of technological change, often viewed as chronological stages, involving *invention, innovation,* and *diffusion.* Schumpeterian Economics and The Trilogy Of 'Invention-Innovation-Diffusion. See: https://www.ischool.utexas.edu/~darius/17-Schumpeter-innovation.pdf
4. Zukis, B., Information technology and cybersecurity governance in a digital world, In R. Leblanc (ed.). *The Handbook of Board Governance.* Wiley Publishing, 2015. Other terms may be used in your firm.
5. PI is defined in section Section 1798.140(o) (1) of the CCPA, see https://www.socalinternetlawyer.com/california-consumer-privacy-act-personal-information-definition/ For more information see the CCPA law found at: https://leginfo.legislature.ca.gov/faces/billTextClient.xhtml?bill_id=201720180AB375
6. Culnan, M. J., & Clark. C. (2009). How ethics can enhance organizational privacy: lessons from the choicepoint and TJX data breaches. *MIS Quarterly*, 673–687.

7. Greenaway, K. E., and Chan, Y. E. 2005. Theoretical Explanations of Firms' Information Privacy Behaviors, *Journal of the Association for Information Systems* (6:6), pp. 171–198.
8. Culnan, M. J. and Clark C. (2009). How ethics can enhance information security: Lessons from the ChoicePoint and TJX Data breaches. *Management Information Systems Quarterly*, 33(4): 673–688.
9. PwC 2018. The Global State of Information Security. See: https://www.pwc.com/us/en/services/consulting/cybersecurity/library/information-security-survey.html
10. Much of this section is adapted from Clark, C. E., Chang, K. K. & Melvin, S.P. (2020), Business & Society: Ethical, Legal and Digital Environments, 1e. Sage Publications.
11. For more information see the CCPA law found at: https://leginfo.legislature.ca.gov/faces/billTextClient.xhtml?bill_id=201720180AB375
12. ComplianceWeek Webinar. Forget me not: business challenges over rights to erasure and threats to AI. March 28, 2019.
13. Regulation (EU) 2016/679 (General Data Protection Regulation) is arranged by chapters, sections, and articles. See: https://advisera.com/eugdpracademy/gdpr/
14. Information Technology & Innovation Foundation, 2017. The Economics of "Opt-Out" Versus "Opt-In" Privacy Rules. See: https://itif.org/publications/2017/10/06/economics-opt-out-versus-opt-in-privacy-rules
15. Pew Research Center, 2016. See: https://www.pewresearch.org/fact-tank/2016/09/21/the-state-of-privacy-in-america/
16. Grupo is a fictitious company based on a composite of many social media companies.
17. Valentine, E., De Haes, S., & Timbrell, G. (2016). The board's role in the governance of enterprise information and technology. *The Handbook of Board Governance: A Comprehensive Guide for Public, Private and Not-for-Profit Board Members*, 574–596.
18. NACD Risk Oversight Advisory Council: Current and Emerging Practices in Cyber-Risk Oversight (June 2019). See: https://www.nacdonline.org/insights/content.cfm?ItemNumber=66907
19. The Harris Poll. See: https://theharrispoll.com/ibm-survey-reveals-consumers-want-businesses-to-do-more-to-actively-protect-their-data/

20. Ghosh, D., What you need to know about California's new data privacy law, *Harvard Business Review*, July 11, 2018.
21. Audit Committee Leadership Network, ALCN Viewpoints: Board Oversight of Privacy, April 2019
22. As recommended by NACD Risk Oversight Advisory Council. See more at: https://www.nacdonline.org/insights/publications.cfm?ItemNumber=65591
23. As recommended by NACD Risk Oversight Advisory Council. See more at: https://www.nacdonline.org/insights/publications.cfm?ItemNumber=65591

CONCLUSION

This book underscores the need for a different approach to ethics in our workplaces and more specifically the significant and unique work of the board of directors. Board members need to build moral muscle memory so they develop the competence and confidence to act ethically even when forces compel them to act otherwise.

The GVV framework is intended to help *you*, today's board member, to learn how to design a strategy for acting when you know – and want to do – what is right. By placing yourself in various board challenges, outlined in this book, and starting from the presumption that you know what the right action is, you can focus on developing a plan or decision tree to *act* on your values rather than simply discussing your values.

The GVV approach helps you learn to identify the shareholders' and stakeholders' interests, in order to anticipate common reasons you will encounter from others when you speak out, and to prepare actions and scripts for responding to such rationalizations. Some of the most common reasons and rationalizations offered and discussed throughout this book include: (1) standard practice (2) materiality (3) locus of responsibility and (4) locus of loyalty.

Similarly, each board challenge presents a handful of strategies that can help counter these rationalizations. As you work through these board challenges, you may begin to see patterns. Through practice with these real-life board challenges, you can begin to believe it's possible to act ethically and thrive in the boardroom. These skills allow you to take pride in finding viable solutions that result in gains for everyone rather than dead-end arguments that result in stilted conversations and resentments. Simply put, it can help to improve the sub-optimal board dynamics you may be currently at the mercy of. So, please share this book with your fellow board members and the CEO.

As you continue to learn from this book, it's important to remember that taking action does not always have to involve a big leap. Action can take a variety of forms from gathering research, presenting alternatives, asking questions to probe and clarify positions, identifying key decision makers, and mirroring what others say in order to reframe it. Through flexing your moral muscle, you can develop additional strategies to add to your own toolkit for voicing values over time.

Moral muscle, and the knowledge you possess it, is one of those skills we all need in order to effectively function in the global workplace. Boards of directors are in a unique position to affect change in the business world. In most situations, directors are at the forefront of corporate accountability and judgment. This position, literally, gives board members an opportunity to shape others' actions – especially those of management and other key stakeholders.

This book is based on the belief that the vast majority of us want to do what is right and ethical. The pressures of the situation, though, often distort our thinking. We need to remind ourselves that, in the end, what is ethical is also what is best for the company, its stakeholders and our society.

DEFINITIONS

Note: these words are *italicized* in book

Artificial intelligence Machine-based learning involving adaptive mechanisms that enable computers to learn from example, experience and analogy.

Compensation committee A core board of director committee responsible for all elements of the company's executive compensation and human capital management, including establishing competitive salary levels and crafting appropriate short- and long-term incentives that are intended to drive performance.

Corporate governance Specifies the distribution of rights and responsibilities among various corporate participants including board members, executives, shareholders and other stakeholders; it spells out the rules and procedures for making decisions on corporate affairs (see page 17 for definitions from difference perspectives).

Director selection process The formal or informal process by which individuals are identified and screened for a position on a corporate board.

Duty of care The director requirement to exercise care, diligence and skill that a person in a similar position would reasonably believe is appropriate under similar circumstances.

Duty of confidentiality Directors are prohibited from using insider information (i.e., proprietary information that is of competitive or commercial value to the corporation, or information about its finances, operations and strategy).

Duty of loyalty The director requirement to act honestly and in good faith with a view to the best interests of the company, obligating a director to act independently (e.g., of the CEO's personal interests or their own personal interests).

Gray director A director who lacks perceived independence for one or more reasons but are nonetheless independent for regulatory purposes.

Fiduciary duty The trust that one party will act in the best interests of another, owing them a duty of loyalty and care.

Fintech Term used to refer to innovations in the financial and technology crossover space and typically refers to companies or services that use technology to provide financial services to businesses or consumers.

Locus of loyalty rationalization Recognizing that loyalties can conflict, using this rationalization assumes that loyalty to one group necessarily means disloyalty to another group. Sometimes, people express this rationalization something like: "I don't want to harm [person x] but I know this isn't fair to [person y]".

Locus of responsibility rationalization Refers to our sense of who we think should act in a given situation or who is requiring us to act in a situation. It is best captured by the statements "It is not my problem" or "I'm just following orders". This rationalization usually reduces your personal accountability because you think your actions result from some authority figure who has the control.

Materiality rationalization Refers to making the argument that an action is not material, it doesn't matter, it is insubstantial, it does not hurt anyone, or it does not make a difference in the long run. Framing the question in terms of materiality shifts the focus from the action to its consequences and it also minimizes those consequences.

Nominating committee One of the customary standing committees (along with the audit and compensation committees), whose main role is to independently evaluate and nominate perspective candidates for the board of directors and in some cases choose the lead director of the entire board and accept or deny director resignations. It is required to be composed of either entirely or mostly of independent directors, depending on the jurisdiction.

Personal information Information that identifies, relates to, describes, is capable of being associated with, or could reasonably be linked, directly or indirectly, with a particular consumer or household.

Privacy A multidimensional concept relating broadly to confidentiality of personal information.

Security A company's specific efforts to protect personal information.

Shareholder A person, group or organization owning one or more shares of stock in a corporation.

Shareholder perspective The perception that shareholders, as a stakeholder group, deserve primacy because they are the foundation of a firm's survival and directly relevant to the firm's core economic interest.

Stake A kind of interest in or claim on something of value.

Standard practice rationalization Is best captured by the statement, "Everyone does it". This argument assumes that an action is acceptable simply because the majority of the people engage in it or because it is something that has been done for a long period of time.

Stakeholder Any identifiable group or individual who can affect the achievement of an organization's objectives or who is affected by the achievement of an organization's objectives. Also defined as a person who has an interest or concern (not necessarily financial) in the success or failure of an organization, system, plan, or strategy or who is affected by a course of action.

Stakeholder perspective The perception that multiple and varied groups affect and are affected by the firm and that it is important to create value for society beyond a pure monetary benefit for shareholders.

INDEX

Note: Page numbers in *italics* indicate figures and with "n" indicate endnote in the text.